Pritam Uberoi's
INDIAN
COOKERY

Pritam Uberoi's
INDIAN
COOKERY

STERLING PUBLISHERS PRIVATE LIMITED

STERLING PUBLISHERS PRIVATE LIMITED
L-10, Green Park Extension, New Delhi-110016

Indian Cookery
©1991, Pritam Uberoi
First Edition 1987
Reprint 1990, 1991, 1992

PRINTED IN INDIA

Published by S.K. Ghai, Managing Director, Sterling Publishers Pvt. Ltd., L-10, Green Park Extension, New Delhi-110016.
Printed at Ram Printograph (India), C-114, Okhla Phase-I, New Delhi-110020.

INTRODUCTION

Since my childhood, I remember, I took interest in cooking. Later I devoted myself to lecturing and teaching in colleges, and held many demonstrations on the art of cooking and for charity programmes. At the request of my pupils and well-wishers, I have ventured on a task which I sincerely hope will be of material benefit not only to Indian housewives but also to housewives abroad. Every recipe in this book can be used in any country by any housewife.

I had my education at Mahila Mahavidyalaya College, Lahore, and subsequently at Lady Irwin College, Delhi. I married Shri G.S. Uberoi, a Sikh businessman, in 1943. He is very fond of good food, and in fact, has always been encouraging me to try new dishes which helped me immensely at a later stage. Mrs Tara Bai, ex-Director of Lady Irwin College, asked me to share my knowledge of cooking with the students of Lady Irwin College. My dedication resulted in my appoinment as Director, Delhi School of Cookery. Although an introvert by nature and religious in views, I have ambitious plans of transforming young girls into accomplished wives and thus endear them to their husbands. For, I am convinced, to use a cliche, that the easy way to a man's heart is through his stomach. It is a universal truth unchanged by time. Good food at home prevents many tensions of marital life, destroys the temptation to 'eat out' in the restaurants, thereby providing an economic solution to many household problems, in addition to healthy nourishment.

Vegetarian cakes and puddings mentioned in this book are my special innovations. The western dishes have also been admired by the connoisseurs. Some specially prepared dishes displayed at the 15th World Vegetarian Conference held at Delhi in 1957, were highly appreciated by the press and the public. There, my eldest daughter Jasmin (at that time just fourteen), was awarded the first prize for a salad preparation. My younger daughter Nimi, also got the first prize in canning and preservation from the Government of India's Community Canning and Preservation Centre. My children, one son and two daughters, have always provided constructive criticism on numerous culinary experiments in my kitchen. I am highly grateful to them. Finally, I wish to thank all those who have encouraged me in writing the non-vegetarian and vegetarian cookery books.

B-5/5 Safdarjang Enclave
New Delhi-110029

(Mrs) Pritam Uberoi

GLOSSARY

English	Hindustani
Almond	*Badam*
Alum	*Phitkari*
Aniseed	*Saunf*
Apricots	*Khurmani*
*Asafoetida	*Heeng*
Baking powder	*Pakane ka soda*
Bay leaf	*Tej patta*
Beans	*Sem*
Beetroot	*Chukander*
Black pepper	*Kali mirch*
Bottle gourd	*Louki, ghia*
Brinjal	*Baingan*
Buttermilk	*Lassi, ghol*
Cabbage	*Band gobhi*
Capsicum	*Simla mirch, Bara mirch*
Cardamom	*Elaichi*
Carrot	*Gajar*
Castor sugar	*Powder or Pisi cheenee*
Cashewnuts	*Kaju*
Caraway	*Ajwain*
Cayenne	*Lal mirchi*
Cauliflower	*Phool gobhi*
Chapati	*Indian bread*
Cheese	*Vilayati paneer*
Chillies	*Lal mirch*
Cinnamon	*Dalchini*
Citric acid	*Tatri*
Clarified Butter	*Ghee*
Cloves	*Laung*
Cooking apple	*Kachcha seb*

*Asafoetida water—Heeng water. Mix one teaspoon ground heeng into one cup hot water.

English	Hindustani
Cochineal	*Sweet gulabi rang*
Coconut	*Narial*
Colocasia	*Arabi*
Coriander leaves	*Hara dhania*
Coriander seeds	*Sukha dhania*
Cottage cheese	*Paneer*
Cucumber	*Kheera*
Cumin seeds	*Zeera*
Curd	*Dahi*
Dates	*Khajur*
Drumsticks	*Sahjan ki phali, singi*
Dried ginger	*Sonth*
Dry breadcrumbs	*Sookhi double roti ka choora*
Dry mango powder	*Amchoor*
Fenugreek	*Methi*
Flour	*Maida*
French beans	*Fras beans*
Garlic	*Lehsoon*
Ginger	*Adarak*
Gram	*Chana*
Gram dal	*Chana ki dal*
Gram flour	*Besan*
Grapes	*Angoor*
Green chilli	*Hari mirch*
Green pumpkin	*Ghia, lauki, kaddu*
Griddle	*Tawa*
Groundnut oil	*Moongphali tel*
Guchhi	*Black mushrooms*
Icing sugar	*Icing cheenee*
Jaggery	*Gur*
Kewara essence	*Indian kewara essence*
Milk solidified by prolonged cooking	*Khoya*
Lady's fingers	*Bhindi*
Lemon	*Neembu*
Lemon rind	*Neembu ka chhilka*
Lentils	*Dal*
Mace	*Jawitri*

English	Hindustani
Mango	*Aam*
Mango powder	*Amchoor*
Melon seeds	*Magaz*
Mint	*Pudina*
Mustard	*Rai*
Mustard oil	*Sarson tel*
Nutmeg	*Jaiphal*
Onion	*Pyaz*
Onion seeds	*Kalaunji*
Papaya	*Papita*
Peas	*Matar*
Peppercorn	*Sabut kali mirch*
Peaches	*Aadu*
Pickle	*Achar*
Pistachio	*Pista*
Pomegranate	*Anardana*
Poppy seeds	*Khus khus*
Radish	*Mooli*
Raisins	*Kismis*
Red chilli powder	*Kashmiri mirch powder*
Rice	*Chawal*
Rose water	*Gulab jal*
Saffron	*Kesar*
Salt	*Namak*
Sesamum	*Til*
Semolina	*Sooji, rawa*
Sevian	*Vermicelli*
Soft breadcrumbs	*Taji double roti ka choora*
Spinach	*Palak*
Spring onion	*Hara pyaz*
Sugar	*Cheenee*
Sultana	*Munakka (bara kismis)*
Sweet potato	*Shakarkandi*
Tamarind	*Imli*
Turnip	*Shalgam*
Turmeric	*Haldi*
Thymol seeds	*Ajwain*
Vinegar	*Sirka*
White gram	*Kabli chana, safed chana*
White mushrooms	*Dhingri*
White pumpkin	*Petha*
Wholewheat flour	*Gehun ka atta*

Dictionary of Cookery Words

Bake Cook by dry heat in an oven or tandoor (Indian oven).

Batter A mixture of flour and water or milk—thin enough to pour.

Beat Mix vigorously with a spoon, wire beater or egg beater, to enclose air in the food.

Blanch Remove skins of fruit or nuts by dipping into boiling water.

Blend Mix the ingredients thoroughly.

Boil Cook in boiling water or other liquid in which bubbles are rising on the surface and steam is given off.

Brush Spread thinly.

Caramel syrup Melt sugar to a brown colour by heating. It is only used for colouring and flavouring.

Chill Allow to become thoroughly cold but not frozen.

Chop Cut into very small pieces with a sharp knife or chopper.

Cream Mix two ingredients together, such as, butter or ghee with sugar until the mixture is light and fluffy.

Deep frying Cook in hot ghee or oil deep enough to float the food.

Dissolve Cause the dry ingredients to transform into liquid.

Dust	Sprinkle or coat lightly with flour.
Fold in	Mix by a gentle motion. Proper folding in prevents loss of air.
Fondant	Sugar syrup cooked to the soft ball stage, cooled and kneaded to a creamy mass.
Garnish	To decorate.
Ghee	It is obtained by melting butter and boiling to free it from water and strained through a muslin cloth. This is unknown outside India.
Grate	Shred food by rubbing against a grater.
Mince	Cut with a sharp knife into very small pieces.
Peel	Remove outer covering as from peaches, tomatoes, etc.
Sift	Pass through a sieve.
Simmer	Cook in water on very low fire below the boiling point.
Stir	Mix with a spoon using circular motion.
Shallow frying	Cook in small amount of ghee.
Soak	Immerse in liquid for sometime.
Whip	Beat rapidly.
Ground Spices	

1 cup cumin seeds

$\frac{1}{2}$ cup coriander seeds

$\frac{1}{2}$" piece cinnamon

6 big cardamoms

12 cloves

Grind all the spices finely and keep in an airtight bottle.

Important Hints

Instead of ghee any kind of fat can be used such as dripping. hard margarine, suet or any edible oil.

Garlic powder can be used instead of fresh garlic; $\frac{1}{4}$ teaspoon garlic powder is equal to 4 garlic flakes.

$\frac{1}{2}$ tin spinach is equal to 2 lbs spinach.

1 teaspoon dry ginger is equal to 2 teaspoons fresh ginger (but soak dry ginger in $\frac{1}{4}$ cup water).

Curries should always be cooked slowly to extract all the richness and flavour of the spices.

Do not use soda bicarbonate for softening food as it destroys the vitamins.

Do not use large amount of water for cooking vegetables.

Scrape the skins of vegetables, and do not peel them as Mrs Peeler is the vitamin stealer.

Cook fleshy foods till tender, on low fire. Excessive cooking destroys the food value.

> 6 ozs sugar = 1 teacup
> 5 ozs milk or water = 1 teacup
> 4 ozs flour = 1 cup packed tightly
> 3 teaspoons ghee = 1 oz
> 4 teaspoons sugar = 1 oz
> 4 teaspoons butter = 1 oz
> 6 teaspoons maida = 1 oz

CONTENTS

7. RAITA

8. SNACKS

9. CHICKEN, FISH, MUTTON AND PORK PREPARATIONS

1

SOUPS

CARROT CREAM SOUP
(Serves 8)

12 ozs chopped carrots (360 grams)
1 spring onion
3 ozs boiled rice (90 grams)
20 ozs milk (4 teacups)
20 ozs water (4 teacups)
1 teaspoon sugar
1 oz butter (30 grams)
1 teaspoon chopped coriander leaves
3 teaspoons cornflour
Salt to taste
½ teaspoon white pepper

Mix the cornflour to a smooth paste with a little milk. Boil the rest of the milk and stir in cornflour paste. Cook until it becomes a little thick. Keep this aside. Cook chopped carrots and onion in butter, on very low fire, for five minutes. Be careful that the carrots do not become brown. Add the milk stock, boiled rice, salt, pepper, sugar, water and coriander. Bring to boil and simmer, with lid on, for 35 to 40 minutes. Pass through a sieve; reheat and then remove from the fire and add 1 oz butter. Serve hot. (If carrot soup is too thick, mix a little milk with it).

MIXED VEGETABLE SOUP
(Serves 6)

6 cups water

4 small potatoes, cubed

2 medium onions, sliced

2 carrots, diced

1½ ozs beans (45 grams)

3 large tomatoes, skinned and chopped

1 clove

2 tablespoons split green peas

¼ teacup butter

4 teaspoons grated cheese

4 level teaspoons flour

½ teaspoon salt

White pepper to taste

Combine all the ingredients except the butter and cheese in a large soup pan. Cover the pan and boil gently till tender. Then strain it. Heat the butter. Fry the flour for a few minutes without browning, add the strained soup and stir for five minutes. Remove from the fire and sprinkle the cheese. Serve at lunch or dinner.

ALMOND SOUP WITH CREAM
(Serves 8)

Stock

8 ozs mutton ribs (250 grams)
1 small piece ginger
1 bay leaf
10 peppercorns
1 small piece onion
12 cups water
10 crushed almonds

Cook the mutton ribs with all the ingredients till quite tender and the liquid is reduced to 8 cups. Strain. Heat the stock with crushed almonds.

Soup

12 level teaspoons flour
½ oz butter
⅓ cup cream
A little cornflour (1 or 2 teaspoons)
Salt to taste
White pepper to taste

Fry the flour in butter, till it is still white, on very low fire. Add the stock with almonds and stir it till it becomes slightly thick. If it is thin, mix cornflour in ¼ cup of water and add it to the soup and cook further till thick Mix salt and pepper, pour in cups and add 1 teaspoon cream in each cup. Serve hot.

TOMATO CREAM SOUP

(Serves 8)

3 lbs tomatoes (1½ kg)
2 onions
2 bay leaves
6 cloves
2 teaspoons sugar
Water to cover the tomatoes
Salt to taste

Chop the onions. Put the tomatoes, chopped onions, bay leaves, salt, cloves and water in a pan and cook until tender and a little thick. Remove from the fire, cool and pass through a sieve.

Cream
½ oz butter (15 grams)
3 teaspoons flour
¼ teaspoon salt
⅛ teaspoon white pepper
1 teacup milk

Heat the butter, fry the flour in it till golden brown; add the milk slowly, stirring constantly, till a little thick and smooth. Pass it through a sieve and add salt, pepper, cream and mix well. Heat the above strained tomato pulp and add the strained cream mixture and mix the two lightly. Serve hot at dinner or lunch with croutons.

Note : Do not heat the soup after mixing cream.

CHICKEN CREAM SOUP
(Serves 10)

Stock

250 grams chicken bones and 4 haunches of lamb
2 chicken breasts
3 bay leaves
1 big onion
1 big slice of ginger
1 medium potato
14 cups water

Put all the ingredients in a pan and cook until the chicken breasts are tender. Take out the other things except the chicken breasts from the stock and again cook on a low fire till the bones are quite tender. Mash the meat and strain it.

Soup

2 pints stock (6 teacups)
8 level teaspoons flour
1 oz butter (3 teaspoons)
1½ tablespoons milk
2 ozs cream (¼ cup)
Salt and pepper to taste

Melt the butter in a pan and fry the flour for 2 minutes without browning it. Add the stock and cook till a little thick. Mix small pieces of boiled chicken breast, milk, salt and pepper. Pour into soup dishes and mix lightly one teaspoon cream in each soup dish.

5

2

RICE AND PULAO

SHAH JAHANI BIRIANI
(Serves 6)

1 lb rice ($\frac{1}{2}$ kg)
1 lb stock (5 teacups)
2 big cardamoms
3 green cardamoms
1 garlic pod
1″ piece ginger
$\frac{1}{2}$ cinnamon
4 cloves
2 teaspoons aniseed
2 teaspoons coriander seeds (tie them in a muslin cloth)
1 medium thinly sliced onion
1 teaspoon red chilli powder
2 teaspoons cumin powder
3 teaspoons salt
1 tablespoon ghee
1 cup milk
5 cashewnuts or almonds
$\frac{1}{4}$ teaspoon grated nutmeg
2 teaspoons kewara flavour

6

1 to 2 bay leaves
$\frac{1}{4}$ teaspoon yellow colour
$\frac{1}{4}$ teaspoon orange colour
1 lb mutton ribs ($\frac{1}{2}$kg)
$\frac{3}{4}$ teacup ghee
Silver leaves for decoration

Boil the meat with 3 teaspoons salt, garlic pod, ginger, cloves, cinnamon, cardamoms, green cardamoms and the muslin cloth containing aniseeds and coriander seeds in 10 cups of water till it becomes tender. Strain and remove the whole spices, garlic pod and the muslin bag. Soak the rice for 20 minutes. Fry the slices of onion in ghee with bay leaf till light brown. Add the stock, cumin powder, salt, red chilli powder, fried cashewnuts (broken into half) and mutton ribs and cook till it boils. Add milk and then soaked rice and mix them well. Cook it without stirring till the water is evaporated. Put it on very low fire till rice becomes tender. Then mix grated nutmeg and kewara flavour. Pour the colours separately with a teaspoon on the rice and leave on the fire for a few more minutes. Remove from the fire and keep aside for 10 minutes. Serve it in an oval dish and decorate with silver leaves.

BOILED RICE (BY EVAPORATION)
(Serves 3)

8 ozs rice (250 grams)
1 teaspoon salt
1 lb water (3 teacups)

Pick, wash and soak rice for 25 minutes. Boil water with salt, then add rice and mix well. Cover the degchi and cook gently till the rice is cooked and water is absorbed completely leaving each grain separate.

SHAHI SWEET PULAO
(Serves 8)

1 lb rice (500 grams)
4 ozs ghee (125 grams)
1½ pints water (6 teacups)
9 ozs sugar (270 grams)
1 oz cherries (30 grams)
1 oz almonds (30 grams)
½ oz raisins (15 grams)
½ oz pistachios (15 grams)
6 silver leaves
6 green cardamoms
4-5 ozs khoya (125-150 grams)
3 tablespoons castor sugar
½ teaspoon kewara essence
½ teaspoon of each colour —orange, green, red and yellow.

Pick, wash and soak the rice for 25 minutes. Make the syrup with sugar and 6 ozs water. Remove from the fire and keep aside. Heat the ghee, add crushed green cardamoms, rice and 24 ozs water. When the water is absorbed add the syrup. Simmer until the rice is tender and the syrup has been absorbed, then pour colours separately on the rice. Let the rice remain on fire for 2 more minutes. Remove from the fire, add khoya mixed with castor sugar and kewara and mix the rice well. Keep it covered. Chop the cherries, almonds and pistachios for decoration. Serve the rice in an oval plate. Decorate with silver leaves, almonds, pistachios and cherries. Serve hot.

CHANA DAL PULAO
(Serves 6)

1 lb rice (500 grams)
1½ pints water (6 teacups)
4 to 6 ozs chana dal (125-180 grams)
¼ teaspoon red chilli powder
1 teaspoon peppercorns
4 cloves
1 onion, sliced
1″ cinnamon piece
1 bay leaf
2 big cardamoms
1 teaspoon black cumin seeds
Salt to taste
5 ozs ghee (150 grams)

Soak the dal for 15 minutes and boil in salted water until tender, and each grain is separate. Put in a strainer to remove excess water. Keep the dal aside. Fry the onion slices with bay leaf, cloves, cinnamon and cardamoms, until brown. Add the water, rice, salt, peppercorns, red chilli powder and cumin seeds and cook on medium fire until tender and water is absorbed. Fry the boiled dal in 1 oz ghee for a few minutes, and mix it lightly into cooked rice. Serve hot.

GUCHHI PULAO
(Serves 6)

1 lb rice (500 grams)
1½ pints water (6 teacups)
2 ozs guchhi (60 grams)
1 teaspoon coarsely ground black cumin seeds
½ teaspoon coarsely ground cinnamon
¼ teaspoon coarsely ground cloves
½ teaspoon red chilli powder
1 medium onion, sliced
5 ozs ghee (150 gms)
Salt to taste

Soak the guchhi overnight and then wash thoroughly. Wash and soak the rice for 15 minutes. Heat the ghee with coarsely ground spices, add water and boil. Now add the rice, salt, red chilli powder and guchhi and cook on medium fire until tender and water is absorbed. Fry the onion slices until golden brown and crisp. Garnish the pulao with them. Serve hot. If tinned black mushrooms are used, they should not be soaked overnight.

CARROT PULAO
(Serves 8)

1 lb rice (500 grams)
5 ozs ghee (150 grams)
10 ozs sugar (300 grams)
6 green cardamoms
1½ pints water (6 teacups)
1 lb carrots (500 grams)
2 teaspoons kewara flavour
1 oz raisins (30 grams)
3 silver leaves
½ teaspoon yellow colour
½ oz pistachios (15 grams), slivered

Scrape the carrots and grate them. Prepare a syrup with sugar, 8 ozs water and grated carrots in a degchi and cook until carrots are half tender. Heat the ghee, add soaked rice, cardamoms, the remaining water and yellow colour and cook until water is absorbed. Now add the syrup with carrots, raisins and cook until rice is tender. Sprinkle kewara flavour and decorate with silver leaves and pistachios. If the rice is not completely cooked, cover them with a wet cloth and cover the degchi tightly. Keep on a very low fire or over a pan of hot water. Serve hot with dinner or lunch.

11

FISH KABAB PULAO
(Serves 6)

1 lb rice ($\frac{1}{2}$ kg)
1 big onion
1$\frac{1}{2}$ pints fish stock (6 teacups)
3 ground cloves
$\frac{1}{2}$ teaspoon red chilli powder
1 teaspoon white cumin seeds
$\frac{1}{2}$ teaspoon coarsely ground cinnamon
2 big ground cardamoms
4 to 5 ozs ghee ($\frac{1}{2}$ teacup)
Salt to taste

Fish Kababs
1 lb fish ($\frac{1}{2}$ kg)
1$\frac{1}{2}$ teaspoons ground spices
4 small ginger pieces
1 small onion
2 green chillies
$\frac{3}{4}$ teaspoon black pepper
2 egg whites
Ghee for deep frying

Boil the fish in 1$\frac{1}{2}$ pints water with one teaspoon salt until tender. Drain the fish pieces and retain the stock. Cool the pieces, remove bones and skin and mash. Add ground spices, salt, chopped green chillies, ginger and onion and mix well. Make small round balls and dip in lightly beaten egg whites. Fry in hot ghee until light brown. Drain on paper. Soak the rice for 15 mts. Cut the onion into thin slices and fry in ghee until brown. Add the fish stock, salt, chilli powder, ground cumin seeds, cinnamon, cardamoms, cloves and rice. Cook until tender. Remove from the fire and put fried fish balls on the rice Cover the degchi for 15 minutes. Serve hot.

12

SHAHI KORMA CHICKEN PULAO
(Serves 6)

½ medium chicken
1 lb rice (½ kg)
1½ pints stock (6 teacups)
4 ozs curd (¾ cup)
2 teaspoons coriander powder
1 teaspoon cumin powder
¼ teaspoon ground cloves
6 green cardamoms
1 small piece ground cinnamon
5 ozs ghee (½ teacup)
1 onion
2 ozs cashewnuts (60 grams)
⅛ teaspoon grated nutmeg
1 tomato
Salt to taste
½ teaspoon red chilli powder

Fry medium-sized pieces of boiled chicken with ground spices, and, whole cardamoms, until golden brown. Add the curd, red chilli powder and chopped tomato without skin and stir for a few minutes. Add the soaked rice, salt, stock and grated nutmeg and cook until tender, and water is absorbed. Garnish with fried and crisp onion rings and lightly browned cashewnuts.

13

MUTTON BIRIANI
(Serves 6)

1 lb mutton ($\frac{1}{2}$ kg)
1 lb rice ($\frac{1}{2}$ kg)
Water to cover the meat
3 bay leaves
3 cloves
1$\frac{1}{2}$ pints stock for rice (6 teacups)
2 small pieces cinnamon
2 big cardamoms
6 green cardamoms
3$\frac{1}{2}$ teaspoons coriander seeds
    (tie in a muslin cloth)
1 teaspoon aniseed
5 ozs ghee ($\frac{1}{2}$ teacup)
20 black peppercorns
4 pieces ginger
1$\frac{1}{2}$ teaspoons white cumin seeds
1 onion
$\frac{1}{4}$ teaspoon nutmeg
$\frac{3}{4}$ teaspoon orange colour
2 teaspoons kewara essence
1 small pod garlic
Salt to taste

Boil the meat with garlic pod and all the spices including aniseed and coriander seeds tied in a cloth except nutmeg, and cook until tender. Fry the chopped onion, add meat and fry for 5 minutes. Add the soaked rice, strained stock and $\frac{1}{2}$ teaspoon orange colour and cook until water has evaporated. Add the grated nutmeg, kewara essence and mix well. Mix $\frac{1}{4}$ teaspoon orange colour in half the rice and keep the degchi covered for 2 minutes. Serve at dinner or lunch.

14

3

PARATHAS, PURIS AND NAN

ORDINARY PARATHA
(Serves 10)

2 lbs wholewheat flour (1 kg)
1 teaspoon salt
6 to 8 ozs ghee (180 grams or 250 grams)

Sift the flour and add a little salt and 1 tablespoon ghee. Rub the ingredients between the palms to mix them thoroughly. Pour a little water at a time and keep on kneading till it binds. and the dough is not too soft. Take small portions of the dough, roll them out into chapatis and smear them with ghee. Fold them up into round balls and roll out once more. Put on a heavy and hot griddle. Bake one side of the parathas and turn over. Add a little ghee from the sides and cook them on a low fire. When ready they should be crisp and light brown. Serve at lunch.

BESAN PARATHA
(Serves 8)

1 lb wholewheat flour (500 grams)

8 ozs besan (250 grams)

½ teaspoon ground red chillies

4 ozs ghee (125 grams)

1 teaspoon coarsely ground coriander seeds

1 teaspoon chopped green chillies

2 teaspoons pomegranate seeds

Salt to taste

Sift both the flours and knead them together with water as for chapati dough. Mix all the above ingredients into the dough except ghee. Make 12 round balls. Roll each ball into a thick round, smear with a little ghee and fold it up into a round ball. Dip the ball into dry wheat flour and roll out into a round thin paratha. Cook both sides of the paratha on a griddle (tawa) and baste well with ghee. Fry till golden brown on both sides. Serve hot at breakfast or lunch with curd.

CAULIFLOWER PARATHA
(Serves 6)

1 lb wholewheat flour (500 grams)
1 big cauliflower
2 teaspoons coarsely ground coriander seeds
4 ozs ghee (125 grams)
2 teaspoons pomegranate seeds
½ teaspoon red chilli powder
½ teaspoon black pepper
Salt to taste

Cut the cauliflower into small pieces. Throw away the hard stalk, use only the upper portion. Put them in a degchi with a little ghee, ground coriander seeds, chilli powder, black pepper, pomegranate seeds and salt. Cook till the water is absorbed and the cauliflower is done. Fry for ten to fifteen minutes, remove from the fire and when slightly cool, grind to a rough paste. Knead the flour with a little salt, into a smooth dough. Take two small portions of the dough, and roll out into two equal sized chapatis. Cover one with a thin layer of the filling (paste) and smear the other with ghee. Place this over the other and pinch the edges. Roll out more, taking care not to break it. Fry as ordinary parathas. Stuffed parathas are served at breakfast with tea, and at lunch with curd.

STUFFED SPINACH AND EGG PURI
(Serves 6)

Filling

8 ozs spinach (250 grams)
1 hard boiled egg
2 chopped green chillies
1 teaspoon coriander powder
Salt to taste

Remove the stems of spinach. Wash and chop. Cook in ¼ cup water till tender and water is absorbed. Mash and mix grated egg, green chillies, coriander powder and salt. Keep aside.

Covering

2¼ cups wholewheat flour
6 teaspoons ghee
¼ teaspoon salt
Ghee for deep frying

Sift the flour and salt and knead it with water until smooth and a little stiff. Cover the dough with a wet cloth and keep for 30 minutes. Knead it again and make small round balls about the size of walnuts. Fill a little of the mixture in each ball and roll out ¼ inch thick. Fry in hot ghee till puffed up, and turn over. Fry till golden brown. Remove from the ghee. Serve hot at breakfast or lunch.

MALAI PURI
(Serves 6)

½ lb flour (250 grams)
2 ozs cream (¼ teacup)
4 ozs milk (¾ teacup)
½ lb potatoes (250 grams)
Ghee for deep frying

Boil the potatoes, peel and mash them to a smooth paste. Mix together the flour, cream, mashed potatoes and a little salt thoroughly. Sprinkle with a little milk and knead into a smooth and fairly hard dough. Divide into small balls and roll out into thick puris. Heat the ghee in a heavy karahi or pan and when smoking hot, reduce the heat and fry the puris to a golden brown colour on both sides. Serve hot at lunch or breakfast with potato bhujia.

DOSA (SOUTH INDIAN)
(Serves 6)

12 ozs rice (360 grams)
6 ozs urad dal (180 grams)
Salt to taste

Soak the rice and dal separately overnight. Strain and grind them separately with the same water in which they were soaked. Add water, if necessary, and make a batter the consistency of pakora batter, mix with salt and keep aside.

Filling

2 lbs potatoes (1 kg)
1 tablespoon ghee or oil
6 oz onion 180 gms
1½ teaspoons mustard seeds
2 teaspoons chopped coriander leaves
3 ozs green chillies (90 grams)
2 teaspoons chopped ginger
Salt to taste

Heat the ghee, and add mustard seeds. When they splutter add the chopped onion, and fry a little. Put one cup water in it and bring it to boil. Now add the coarsely mashed, boiled potatoes, chopped green chillies, ginger, coriander leaves and salt and mix well. Cook for two minutes. Cool it. Heat a little ghee and spread the batter of ground rice and urad dal on a griddle and pour a little ghee round it. Fry one side until light brown. Put a little potato mixture on one side and fold it. Serve hot.

NAN
(Serves 6)

12 ozs flour (360 grams)

4½ ozs wholewheat flour (135 grams)

4½ teaspoons sugar

1 teaspoon salt

6 ozs curd (180 grams)

1¼ teaspoons soda bicarbonate

6 teaspoons melted ghee

2 teaspoons aniseed

2 teaspoons poppy seeds

½ teaspoon onion seeds

Sift the flour and wholewheat flour, and mix salt, sugar, ghee and curd with it. Knead it with a little water until smooth and elastic. Keep it for 15 minutes. Meanwhile heat the tandoor. Dissolve soda in ½ tablespoon water and mix in the dough and knead it again. Make big round balls. Put a little melted ghee and 2 tablespoons curd over each ball. Flatten the balls with the palms of the hands. Make shallow cuts with the back of a knife. Mix aniseed, onion seeds and poppy seeds in a little water and sprinkle over the nans. Stretch each round with hands and then stretch lengthwise from one end. Bake in a moderately hot tandoor and cook till golden in colour. Remove from the tandoor and serve hot. If the nans cannot be served immediately then wrap them up a napkin and keep covered in a degchi so that they remain soft.

BHATHURA
(Serves 10)

1 lb flour (500 grams)
8 ozs semolina (250 grams)
4 ozs yeast (125 grams)
4 ozs soaked and ground urad dal (125 grams)
Ghee for frying

Soak the semolina in 1½ cups water overnight. Add the soaked semolina and yeast to the sifted flour and knead by adding a little warm water until a soft dough is formed. Grease a metal dish with oil, put the dough on it and then sprinkle a little oil over it and keep aside for ½ hour. Make round balls from the dough and fill urad dal mixed with a little salt and red chilli powder in each. Put on a greased metal dish and sprinkle with oil. Leave for another half hour. Flatten with hands and deep fry in hot ghee first on one side and then the other, till light brown. Serve with chana.

Yeast
4 ozs flour (125 grams)
¼ teaspoon soda bicarbonate
1 teacup hot water
2 ozs curd (60 grams)

Mix all the ingredients together and keep for a day.

STUFFED KEEMA PARATHA
(Serves 9)

Filling

8 ozs keema ($\frac{1}{4}$ kg)

2 green chillies

A few coriander leaves

1 teaspoon ginger

2 cloves garlic

2 teaspoons cumin powder

Salt to taste

1 cup water

Cook the keema, chopped ginger and garlic in water till tender and dry. Mix chopped green chillies, coriander leaves cumin powder and salt in it. Fill it in parathas.

Covering

3 cups wheat flour

$\frac{1}{2}$ teaspoon salt

3 teaspoons ghee

1 cup melted ghee for frying

Water for kneading

Mix 3 teaspoons ghee with sifted flour and salt and knead to a soft dough with water. Keep it covered for 25 minutes. Divide into 9 portions. Press each portion in the centre and in the hollow fill cooked keema. Cover the filling entirely. Seal well and flatten a little. Roll into a round chapati and fry on a tawa, using a little ghee, till both sides are golden brown and crisp. Serve hot at breakfast or lunch with curd.

CHICKEN AND EGG PARATHA
(Serves 8)

Paratha

3 cups wholewheat flour

1 teaspoon salt

1 cup ghee

Chicken Mixture

2 Chicken breasts (boiled and chopped)

5 to 6 eggs

A few coriander leaves

2 green chillies

1 teaspoon cumin powder

Salt to taste

To prepare chicken mixture beat the eggs, mix all the ingredients and keep aside.

Knead the sifted flour and salt with a little water/and 4 teaspoons ghee. Keep it covered with a wet cloth for half hour and again knead it till a soft dough is formed. Take a small portion of the dough, roll out into a chapati and smear with ghee. Fold up into a round ball and roll out once more. Put on heavy and hot tawa, bake one side of the paratha and turn over. Add a little ghee on the sides till it is golden brown and crisp. Pour a little chicken mixture on the top of the crisp paratha, turn over and leave it till egg and chicken mixture is set and golden brown in colour. Serve hot at breakfast.

KEEMA NAN
(Serves 8)

Keema Mixture

1 cup keema
2 green chillies
1 teaspoon coriander powder
Salt to taste
1 egg yolk

Cook all the above ingredients, except the egg, till tender
and dry. Cool, mix with the egg yolk and keep aside.

Nan Dough

3 cups flour
1 cup wholewheat flour
1 egg
3 teaspoons sugar
1 teaspoon salt
1 cup curd
1½ teaspoons soda bicarbonate
6 teaspoons melted ghee
Water to knead the dough

Method is the same as for nan, only omit poppy seeds,
aniseed, and onion seeds. Spread the keema mixed with egg yolk
and serve at lunch.

25

4

C U R R I E S

CHANA DAL CURRY
(Serves 10)

Curry

8 ozs chana dal without husk ($\frac{1}{2}$ kg) soaked and ground

1 lb sour curd (500 grams)

4 pints water (15 teacups)

1 teaspoon red chilli powder

2 teaspoons coriander powder

2 teaspoons ground spices

A tiny piece asafoetida

1 teaspoon turmeric

1 teaspoon pomegranate seeds

5 ozs ghee (150 grams)

A few coriander leaves

Salt to taste

Heat the ghee, fry asafoetida until brown and crush it with a spoon. Fry the ground dal with turmeric for 10 minutes. Add the curd beaten with water and stir it until it boils. Add the pakoras and all the spices, salt and red chilli powder and cook on a low fire until thick and pakoras become soft. Sprinkle coriander leaves and serve hot at lunch or dinner with rice or chapatis. (Make the curry thick for chapatis and thin for rice.)

Pakoras

8 ozs chana dal ($\frac{1}{4}$ kg)
1 teaspoon red chilli powder
1 teaspoon chopped fresh ginger
1 teaspoon chopped coriander leaves
1 teaspoon chopped onion
1 teaspoon chopped green chillies
1 teaspoon ground spices
1 teaspoon coarsely ground coriander
Salt to taste
Ghee for deep frying

Soak the chana dal overnight. Drain and grind it finely. Divide the ground dal into half. In one portion mix all the above ingredients of pakoras. Heat the ghee, drop the mixture with a teaspoon or hand and fry until nicely browned. Keep aside.

MUKUND CURRY
(Serves 6)

2 lbs wholewheat flour (1 kg)
½ teaspoon turmeric
1 teaspoon salt
4 onions
6 garlic cloves
2 tomatoes
2 teaspoons fresh ground ginger
A few coriander leaves
1 teaspoon red chilli powder
2 teaspoons ground spices
1 lb peas (½ kg)
Salt to taste
3 tablespoons ghee

Knead the flour as for chapatis and keep aside for 15 mts. Wash the dough several times in water until it becomes elastic. Boil water with one teaspoonful of salt and add the elastic atta and cook until it increases to twice its size. Drain the water and cool it. Squeeze out the water and cut it into small pieces. Fry in ghee till light brown.

Now fry chopped onion and garlic until it becomes brown. Add the chopped tomatoes, ground ginger, ½ teaspoon turmeric, red chilli powder, salt and ground spices and stir constantly until a thick gravy is formed. Add the peas, fried elastic atta and chopped coriander leaves, and fry for two minutes. Add 3 teacups water and cook on a low fire until peas are tender and gravy is reduced to one cup. Serve hot at lunch or dinner.

MUGLAI POTATO KOFTA CURRY
(Serves 8)

Koftas

1 lb potatoes (½ kg)

2 teaspoons ground poppy seeds

1 teaspoons ground fresh ginger

2 teaspoons chopped coriander leaves

2 chopped green chillies

1 teaspoon ground spices

1½ teaspoons cumin powder

4 green cardamoms

Salt to taste

Breadcrumbs for coating

Batter for coating

Ghee for frying

Boil the potatoes in salted water till tender. Cool and grate.
Mix with all the above ground ingredients.

Filling

6 ozs paneer (180 grams)

½ oz yellow colour

Salt to taste

Mash the paneer and mix with yellow colour and salt. Make
round balls of the paneer and cover each ball with potato mixture. Dip in flour batter and coat with breadcrumbs and fry in
ghee till light brown. At the time of serving cut each kofta
into half and put them in a dish. Pour the gravy over them.

ARBI CURRY
(Serves 10)

2 lbs arbi (1 kg)
1 lemon
1½ teaspoons red chilli powder
2 teaspoons ground fresh ginger
1 teacup curd
1 teacup water
8 ozs ghee (¼ kg)
1 teaspoon white cumin powder
2 teaspoons ground spices
1 teaspoon black pepper
Salt to taste

Peel and wash the arbi and prick it with a fork. Sprinkle lemon juice and 1 teaspoon salt on arbi and keep it for one hour. Fry it in hot ghee until golden brown. Now mix in turmeric, ground ginger, ground spices, red chilli powder, black pepper, white cumin powder and salt. Stir it for a few minutes. Beat the curd with water and mix with the fried arbi and cook until a thick gravy is formed. Remove from the fire. Sprinkle chopped coriander leaves. Serve hot at lunch or dinner.

HINDUSTANI BESAN CURRY
(Serves 10)

Curry

1 Ib sour curd ($\frac{1}{2}$ kg)
5 ozs besan (150 grams)
3$\frac{1}{2}$ pints water (2 lit)
1 very small piece asafoetida
2 teaspoons white cumin seeds
2 teaspoons chopped coriander
4 ozs ghee ($\frac{1}{2}$ teacup)
3 teaspoons mango powder
1$\frac{1}{2}$ teaspoons red chilli powder
1 teaspoonful turmeric
1 teaspoon fenugreek seeds
Salt to taste

Beat the curd with 3$\frac{1}{2}$ pints water. Heat the ghee, fry asafoetida, take it out and crush it. In the same ghee fry besan until golden brown. Add ground fried asafoetida, turmeric and the beaten curd gradually and stir it constantly until it boils. Fry fenugreek seeds until golden brown and add into the curd mixture. Now add the ground spices, salt, mango powder, red chilli powder, white cumin seeds and pakoras and cook until thick. Sprinkle chopped coriander and serve hot at lunch or dinner with rice or chapatis. (Make the curry thick for chapatis and thin for rice.)

Pakoras

4 ozs besan (125 grams)
1 big sliced onion
$\frac{1}{4}$ teaspoon red chilli powder
Ghee for deep frying
Water
Salt to taste

Sift the besan, add water to make a batter of dropping consistency. Mix salt, chilli powder and onion slices in it. Heat the ghee and put the mixture in spoonfuls, five to six at a time, and fry till golden brown. Drain the pakoras, and keep aside.

31

KHOYA MATAR CURRY
(Serves 8)

½ lb khoya (¼ kg)

2 lbs peas (1 kg)

6 ozs tomatoes (180 grams)

1 teaspoon asafoetida water

2 teaspoons white cumin powder

1 teaspoon red chilli powder

2 teaspoons ground spices

2 teaspoons chopped coriander leaves

1 teaspoon turmeric

1 teaspoon fresh ground ginger

1 oz fresh coconut (30 grams)

5 ozs ghee (⅓ cup)

Salt to taste

Heat the ghee. Put one teaspoon asafoetida water. Add the khoya and stir with a flat spoon until it is brown. Add the peas, red chilli powder, white cumin powder, turmeric, ground ginger, salt, ground coconut and cover the degchi. Fry the tomatoes in a frying pan in a little ghee and mix them with khoya and matar. Let it simmer for few minutes until the peas are tender. Put the ground spices last with chopped coriander leaves. Serve hot at dinner or lunch.

MALAI KOFTA CURRY
(Serves 8)

Balls

1 lb potatoes ($\frac{1}{2}$ kg)
2 finely chopped green chillies
$\frac{1}{2}$ teaspoon coriander leaves
1 teaspoon finely chopped fresh ginger
1 teaspoon cumin powder
$\frac{1}{2}$ teaspoon ground spices
Salt to taste
Flour for batter ($\frac{1}{2}$ cup water, $\frac{1}{3}$ cup flour)
Breadcrumbs for coating
Ghee for frying
$\frac{1}{3}$ cup cream or malai (frozen)

Boil the potatoes with 1 teaspoon salt till they become tender. Remove from the fire, cool, peel and grate them. Add ground spices, cumin powder, coriander leaves, green chillies, ginger and salt and mix them well. Make round flat balls with the potato mixture and fill one teaspoon of the malai or cream in each ball. Then dip into the flour batter. Coat with breadcrumbs and fry the balls 3 to 4 at a time in hot ghee till golden brown.

Gravy

1 cup chopped onions

4 garlic cloves

2 teaspoons fresh ground ginger

1 teaspoon red chilli powder

1 teaspoon kasuri methi

1 teaspoon ground spices

1 tablespoon ghee

8 ozs tomatoes ($\frac{1}{4}$ kg)

1 bay leaf

4 green cardamoms

2 teapoons cumin powder

Few coriander leaves

Salt to taste

Fry the onions till golden. Add ground ginger, garlic and $1\frac{1}{2}$ cups water and cook till the water is evaporated. Then add bay leaf, peeled chopped tomatoes, cumin powder, ground spices, red chilli powder, green cardamoms, salt to taste and kasuri methi. Cook till it leaves the ghee. Then add $2\frac{1}{2}$ teacups water and boil down to $\frac{3}{4}$ teacup. Remove from the fire. Put the koftas in a dish and pour the boiling gravy over them. Sprinkle chopped coriander leaves.

SAMBAR (SOUTH INDIAN)
(Serves 8)

8 ozs arhar dal ($\frac{1}{4}$ kg)
1 teaspoon turmeric
2 tablespoons ghee
4 pints water (15 teacups)
2 sliced onions
Salt to taste
2 ozs tamarind (60 grams)
2 teaspoons mustard seeds
3 medium tomatoes
6 ozs drumsticks (180 grams)
4 whole red chillies
1 teaspoon fenugreek seeds
2 teaspoons white cumin seeds
$\frac{1}{2}$ oz kukum (15 grams)

Sambar paste: Grind finely 4 tablespoons dry coriander, 12 black peppercorns, 6 whole red chillies and $\frac{1}{2}$ fresh coconut.

Soak the tamarind and kukum separately Cook arhar dal in water, with turmeric and 1 tablespoon ghee, until tender, and no grain is seen. Cut drumsticks into small pieces and soak in hot water for 10 minutes. Remove from the water and add onions, big pieces of tomatoes and cook for ten minutes. Fry mustard seeds and four red chillies until brown; add fenugreek seeds and fry a little, then add to the dal. Now add tamarind pulp, kukum, salt and sambar paste and cook for ten minutes. If thick then add 2$\frac{1}{2}$ cups of hot water. Add chopped coriander leaves and ground white cumin seeds and cook for 5 minutes. Serve with dosa.

35

SINDHI CURRY
(Serves 8)

3 ozs besan (90 grams)

1 oz kukum (30 grams)

4 ozs ghee for frying besan ($\frac{1}{2}$ teacup)

10 teacups water

3 teaspoons turmeric

A few mint leaves

2 teaspoons fenugreek seeds

2 teaspoons chopped coriander leaves

1 teaspoon white cumin seeds

1 oz ghee for frying fenugreek and cumin seeds ($\frac{1}{8}$ teacup)

$\frac{1}{4}$ oz dry mango pieces

2 ozs tamarind (60 grams)

1 oz ghee for frying mustard ($\frac{1}{8}$ teacup)

6 green chillies

2 teaspoons mustard seeds

4 ozs drumsticks (125 grams)

6 ozs bhein or kamal kakri (180 grams)

6 ozs cauliflower (180 grams)

6 ozs potatoes (180 grams)

6 ozs brinjals (180 grams)

2 ozs peas (60 grams)

Soak the kukum, tamarind and dry mango pieces separately. Fry the besan in ghee until light brown, add water, turmeric, salt and big pieces of bhein. Fry fenugreek seeds and white cumin seeds until light brown and then add into besan. Cook for 10 minutes. Add peas, brinjals, cauliflower and drumsticks, chopped green chillies, 4 whole chillies and potatoes and cook until tender. Add chopped coriander leaves, mint leaves, kukum, tamarind pulp, dry mango pieces and cook for a few minutes. Fry mustard seeds in ghee and add to the curry. Serve hot.

VEGETARIAN NARGISI KOFTA CURRY

(Serves 8)

Koftas

1 lb bhein or kamal kakri ($\frac{1}{2}$ kg)

6 to 8 ozs paneer (180 or 250 grams)

$\frac{1}{4}$ teaspoon yellow colour

2 teaspoons white cumin powder

3 ozs roasted besan ($\frac{3}{4}$ teacup)

2 green chillies

Salt to taste

2 teaspoons chopped ginger

1 teaspoon chopped coriander leaves

Ghee for deep frying

Boil the bhein in salted water till tender. Strain, cool, and mash well. Mix cumin powder, roasted besan, chopped green chillies, ginger, coriander and salt with bhein. Take one-fourth of the paneer, mix yellow colour in it, and rub it till smooth. Make small round balls and fill in each some mashed white paneer. Form into egg shapes. Coat with kamal kakri mixture and deep fry till golden brown. Cool the koftas, cut into half, and keep aside.

Curry

1 cup grated onion
4 garlic cloves
2 teaspoons chopped ginger
1 teaspoon red chilli powder
2 teaspoons white cumin powder
1 teaspoon ground spices
2 cloves
6 blanched almonds
4 green cardamoms
3 big tomatoes
Salt to taste
¾ cup ghee

Fry the grated onion till golden brown, add ground garlic and ginger and 1½ cups water and cook it till dry. Mix all the spices and peeled and chopped tomatoes, red chilli powder and salt; cook, stirring all the time, till it leaves the ghee. Add 4 cups of water and cook it till 1½ cups water is left. Put the gravy in a dish. Arrange koftas in it and sprinkle coriander leaves. Serve at dinner or lunch.

STUFFED EGG CURRY
(Serves 6)

Stuffed Eggs

6 hard boiled eggs

12 ozs spinach (360 grams)

2 green chillies

½ cup milk

1 cup fresh breadcrumbs (very fine)

½ teaspoon ground spices

1 teaspoon cumin powder

A few coriander leaves

1 beaten egg

Dry breadcrumbs for coating

Ghee for frying

Remove the stems of spinach leaves. Wash, chop and cook till tender and water is absorbed. Soak the fresh breadcrumbs in milk for 10 minutes. Cut the boiled eggs lengthwise and remove the yolks. Mix the yolks, ground spices, cumin, few coriander leaves, green chillies, salt and soaked breadcrumbs with cooked spinach. Fill the egg white cases with spinach mixture. Dip into the beaten egg mixed with 3 teaspoons of water, coat with breadcrumbs, and fry till golden brown. Put them in the gravy at the time of serving.

Gravy

1 cup chopped onion
10 ozs peeled and boiled tomatoes (300 grams)
1 tablespoon ghee
2 teaspoons ground ginger
6 garlic cloves
1 teaspoon red chilli powder
1½ teaspoons cumin powder
1½ teaspoons ground spices
Salt to taste

Fry the onion till golden brown. Add ground ginger, garlic and 1½ cups water and cook till the water is evaporated and the onions become tender. Add the peeled and chopped tomatoes, ground spices, salt, red chilli and cumin powder, and cook till it leaves its ghee. Add 2½ cups water and cook till the gravy becomes thick. Put the stuffed eggs in a dish and pour boiling gravy over them. Sprinkle few coriander leaves before serving.

CREAM CHICKEN AND EGG
(Serves 4)

1 chicken breast
3 hard boiled eggs
½ teaspoon white pepper
2½ teaspoons lemon juice
3 teaspoons flour
2 cups milk
½ cup cream
Salt to taste
1 oz butter (3 teaspoons)
3 teaspoons chopped onion
1 firm tomato (for decoration)
1 bay leaf

Boil the chicken with bay leaf till tender. Remove the bones and cut into small pieces. Melt the butter, fry flour and onion for a few minutes. Add the milk and chicken pieces and cook for a few minutes. Add the cream and mix it on the fire. Remove from the fire, mix with salt, lemon juice and small pieces of boiled eggs. Put it hot in a dish and decorate with tomato slices. Serve with bread slices.

CHICKEN JHAL FRAIZE (INDIAN)
(Serves 4)

½ chicken
½ carrot
3 small ginger slices
1 bay leaf
½ tomato
½ cup peas
2 green chillies
1 boiled medium patoto cut into pieces
1 sliced onion
¼ teaspoon black pepper
1 teaspoon chopped coriander leaves
⅛ teaspoon turmeric
¼ teaspoon red chilli powder
2 teaspoons tomato ketchup
Salt to taste
1 tablespoon ghee

Boil the chicken with carrot, peas, bay leaf and ginger slices until tender. Cool and remove the bones. Heat the ghee, fry onion slices and chopped ginger until light brown. Add turmeric, salt, pepper, chopped green chillies, chilli powder, pieces of potato, chicken pieces, carrot, peas, coriander leaves and cook for a few minutes. Add tomato sauce and small pieces of tomato in it. Serve hot at lunch or dinner.

GOANESE CHICKEN CURRY
(Serves 6)

1 medium chicken (1½ lbs)
2 onions (4 ozs)
4 teaspoons coriander powder
6 garlic cloves
2 teaspoons long strips of ginger
2 teaspoons red chilli powder
1 teacup curd
2 teaspoons ground spices
1 teaspoon dry fenugreek leaves
1 teaspoon poppy seeds
6 green cardamoms
5 ozs ghee (½ teacup)
Salt to taste

Cut the chicken into medium pieces. Fry the ground onion, garlic, and whole cardamoms until light brown. Add red chilli powder, curd, chicken pieces and stir until dry. Add ground poppy seeds, fenugreek, ground spices, coriander, ginger strips and salt and sufficient water to cook, on a low fire until tender and gravy is thick. Serve hot at lunch or dinner.

KASHMIRI CHICKEN CURRY
(Serves 6)

1 medium chicken
1 big onion
5 garlic cloves
4 small ginger pieces
5 green cardamoms
1 teaspoon red child powder
1½ cups buttermillk or sour milk
2 medium tomatoes
¼ cup cashewnuts
¼ cup peeled and ground almonds
Salt to taste
5 ozs ghee (½ teacup)
½ cup thick cream

Chop the onion and fry in ghee with cardamoms unit light brown. Add ginger and garlic water (grind garlic and ginger with ½ cup of water and squeeze out the liquid) and stir for 5 minutes. Add the chicken pieces, small pecies of tomatoes and red chilli powder and cook for 5 minutes. Add buttermilk, salt, cashewnuts and almonds. Put enough water to cover and cook over low heat until the chicken is tender. Remove from the fire. At the time of serving pour cream over chicken curry and mix it lightly. Serve at dinner or lunch.

MURG MUSALLAM
(Serves 6)

1 medium chicken
3 medium onions
2 big cardamoms
1 small piece cinnamon
4 green cardamoms
2 small pieces ginger
3 cloves
1 bay leaf
2 tablespoons ghee
2 teaspoons poppy seeds
2 ozs peeled almonds (60 grams)
12 ozs milk ($2\frac{1}{2}$ teacups)
$\frac{1}{4}$ teacup khoya
$2\frac{1}{2}$ teaspoons cornflour
A few drops of kewara essence
1 small piece of coconut
3 green chillies
A few coriander leaves
salt to taste

Cook the chicken with green cardamoms, cloves, onion, ginger, big cardamoms in 2 teacups water until tender. Soak poppy seeds in water. Grind coconut, peeled almonds and soaked poppy seeds finely. Mix the khoya, ground almonds, poppy and coconut with milk and cook for a few minutes. Add the cornflour mixed with $\frac{1}{2}$ cup water into milk until a little thick. Add the chicken without spices, salt, chopped green chillies, coriander leaves and kewara essence and cook for a few minutes. Serve hot at dinner.

NARGISI CHICKEN CURRY
(Serves 6)

2 small chickens
1 lb spinach ($\frac{1}{2}$ kg)
5 ozs ghee ($\frac{1}{2}$ teacup)
2 teaspoons ground cloves
$\frac{1}{2}$ teaspoon black pepper
5 green cardamoms
$\frac{1}{2}$ oz coriander powder (15 grams)
$\frac{1}{2}$ oz ginger (15 grams)
8 garlic cloves
$\frac{1}{2}$ teaspoon saffron
4 ozs onion (120 grams)
1 oz khoya (30 grams)
2 eggs
1 teaspoon red chilli powder
Salt to taste

Heat 3 ozs ghee and fry the chicken pieces until brown.
Remove them from the ghee. Fry finely chopped onion and
garlic in the same ghee until golden brown. Add coriander
powder, salt, red chilli powder, chicken with enough water to
cover and cook on low fire until it is tender. Grind cloves,
cardamoms and ginger to a fine paste and add to the chicken.
Dissolve saffron in a little water and stir into it and fry well
for 10 minutes, Remove the chicken pieces from the masala and
keep aside. In a separate degchi heat the remaining ghee (2 ozs)
and fry washed and chopped spinach leaves and khoya with
the masala from the chicken and cook on low fire until the
spinach is cooked dry. Now place the spinach in a frying
pan, lightly beat the egg and spread it on the spinach. When
the egg sets, place the chicken pieces over it and remove in a
serving dish. Serve at lunch or dinner.

46

BENGALI FISH CURRY

(Serves 8)

1½ lbs Rohu fish (¾ kg)

6 ozs onion (180 grams)

½ teaspoon turmeric

8 ozs tomatoes (240 grams)

20 garlic cloves

6 small pieces ginger

2 teaspoonfuls ground spices

1 tablespoon amchoor

1 teaspoon red chilli powder

Salt to taste

6 ozs ghee (¾ teacup)

Fry ground garlic and onion in a shallow pan until brown. Add 1 teacup water, turmeric, ground ginger, red chilli powder, salt, chopped tomatoes and stir until dry. Add 3 teacups water and boil the gravy. Add medium pieces of fish. Keep the pan uncovered and cook on very low fire until tender and gravy is thick. Mix amchoor and ground spices lightly. Do not stir but only shake the pan occasionally to prevent the fish sticking at the bottom of the pan. Serve hot at lunch or dinner with boiled rice.

FISH VINDALOO CURRY
(Serves 8)

1 lb fish (without bones and skin) ½ kg
½ cup vinegar
1 teaspoon salt
Flour for dusting
Ghee for shallow frying
1 teaspoon cumin powder
½ teaspoon red chilli powder

Cut the cleaned fish into medium pieces. Make a paste of red chilli powder, salt and cumin powder with vinegar and rub into the fish pieces. Keep aside for 10 minutes. Dust with flour and fry in hot ghee till golden brown. Remove from the ghee and keep aside.

Gravy

1 cup grated onion

2 teaspoons chopped ginger

8 garlic cloves

4 medium tomatoes

1 teaspoon red chilli powder

2 teaspoons cumin powder

1 teaspoon coriander powder

3 cloves

$\frac{1}{4}$ cup vinegar

$\frac{1}{2}$ teaspoons ground mustard seeds

2 teaspoons ground poppy seeds

1 cup melted ghee

A few coriander leaves

$\frac{1}{2}$ teaspoon black pepper

Salt to taste

Fry the grated onion till light golden brown. Add one cup water, ground garlic and ginger and cook till dry. Add peeled and chopped tomatoes and all the ground spices and salt and stir till dry. Add 3 cups water, cook till it is reduced to half. Add the fish pieces and vinegar; cook for a few minutes. Sprinkle coriander leaves. Serve at lunch or dinner.

ROGAN JOSH
(Serves 8)

1½ lbs meat (¾ kg)
4 onions
20 cloves garlic
10 ginger slices
2 teaspoons white cumin seeds
2 teaspoons coriander seeds
4 cloves
1½ teaspoons red chilli powder
2 big cardamoms
2 big pieces cinnamon
8 ozs tomatoes (250 grams)
3 to 4 tablespoons ghee
Salt to taste

Fry the chopped onion, garlic, big cardamoms and cinnamon until light brown. Add one cup water, salt, ground ginger and stir until onion is tender. Add the meat and cook till it absorbs its water. Add the peeled and chopped tomatoes, ground spices and stir until dry. Add water and cook on low fire until tender and gravy is thick.

Note: Blanch the tomatoes before peeling.

CAULIFLOWER STUFFED WITH KEEMA
(Serves 6)

1 medium cauliflower

8 ozs keema (250 grams)

8 ozs tomatoes (3 medium)

1 bay leaf

2 teaspoons ground ginger

6 thick garlic cloves

2 green cardamoms

1 teaspoon red chilli powder

2 teaspoons white cumin powder

1 teaspoon ground spices

2 teaspoons ground ginger for cauliflower

2 teaspoons fenugreek leaves

2 tablespoons ghee

1 green chilli

A few coriander leaves

¾ cup grated onion

Soak the cauliflower in enough water with 2 teaspoons salt for 35 minutes. Drain the water and put the cauliflower in a strainer to remove as much of the water as possible. Rub 2 teaspoons ground ginger into it. Then fry it golden brown in a shallow pan containing 1 tablespoon ghee, on all sides. Remove from the ghee. Fry the grated onion till light brown. Add ground garlic, ginger, bay leaf and 1 cup water. Cook till the water is evaporated. Add the peeled and chopped tomatoes, ground spices, white cumin powder, salt, red chilli powder, fenugreek leaves, green cardamoms and keema and cook till dry. Add 3 cups water and cook till the meat is tender. Cook the cauliflower and the keema till tender and gravy becomes thick. Put it in a dish and sprinkle coriander leaves and chopped green chillies before serving.

MUTTON DO PIAZA
(Serves 6)

1 lb meat (½ kg)
10 cloves garlic
8 ozs onion (250 grams)
8 ozs curd
2 small pieces fresh ginger
3 cloves
4 ozs tomatoes (120 grams)
6 peppercorns
2 teaspoons white cumin seeds
6 green cardamoms
4 whole red chillies
1 big cardamom
½" piece cinnamon
1 bay leaf
6 ozs ghee (180 grams)
1 teaspoon red chilli powder
Salt to taste

Cut thin and round slices of onion, chop garlic and cut long and thin slices of ginger. Fry 6 ozs onion until golden brown. Add the meat, salt, red chilli powder, peeled and chopped tomatoes, ginger and garlic and fry till meat is dry. Add the curd, 3 cups water, 2 ozs onion slices, black pepper, whole chillies, bay leaf, cinnamon, white cumin seeds, cloves and cardamoms and cook on a low fire until meat is tender. Serve hot at lunch or dinner.

5

DRY VEGETABLES

LAHORI CHANA
(Serves 16)

2 lbs white chana (1 kg)
4 pints water (15 teacups)
4 level teaspoons soda bicarbonate
4 teaspoons tea (tie in a muslin cloth)
6 big cardamoms
3 bay leaves
1 lb tomatoes (½ kg)
4 ozs ginger in long strips (120 grams)
20 green chillies
A few coriander leaves
5 lemons

Pick and wash the chana. Add the water and soda bicarbonate. Bring it to boil on a medium fire and then simmer it on very low fire, keeping the chana covered with a wet cloth till tender (about 1 hour). Put it in a strainer so that water may trickle down. Retain half the water.

Masala

1 teaspoon red chill powder

3¼ ozs ground spices (100 grams)

3½ ozs ground pomegranate seeds (100 grams)

2 teaspoons black pepper

4 teaspoons fenugreek leaves

8 teaspoons salt

6 ozs ghee (¾ teacup)

Mix all the above ingredients lightly with the boiled chana. Make a well in the chana and put the chana water in it. Then sprinkle with masala. Put green chillies (sliced into half) and round slices of tomatoes, ginger strips and coriander leaves all round the chana. Pour smoking hot ghee over them. Serve with lemon pieces.

SPECIAL SOOKHA CHANA
(Serves 10)

1 lb white chana (½ kg)

2 pieces cinnamon

12 cloves

2 teaspoons soda bicarbonate

6 cardamoms

½ oz ginger (15 grams)

2 pints water (7½ teacup)

2 teaspoons salt

Wash and soak the chana with all the ingredients, except salt, overnight. Boil with salt on low fire until tender. Put in a strainer and remove all the spices.

Masala

4 ozs ginger (120 grams)

4 teaspoons chopped green coriander

6 ozs boiled potatoes (180 grams)

3 lemons

10 green chillies

8 ozs tomatoes (250 grams)

8 ozs butter ghee (1 cup)

$\frac{1}{4}$ teaspoon grated nutmeg

3 teaspoons black pepper

$\frac{1}{2}$ teaspoon ground cloves

2 teaspoons coriander powder

3 teaspoons white cumin powder

4 teaspoons black cumin seeds

$\frac{1}{2}$ teaspoon ground big cardamoms

$\frac{1}{2}$ teaspoon ground cinnamon

$\frac{1}{2}$ oz black salt (15 grams)

3 to 4 teaspoons amchoor

Salt to taste

Mix lightly three-fourths of the ground ingredients, small pieces of potatoes, long slices of ginger, and chopped coriander leaves in chana. Heat the ghee and pour over the chana. Add 1 cup boiling water and mix well. Put the degchi on very low fire for 10 minutes. Sprinkle the rest of the ground spices before serving at dinner or lunch.

STUFFED LADY'S FINGERS
(Serves 5)

1 lb lady's fingers ($\frac{1}{2}$ kg)
1 tablespoon amchoor
1 teaspoon turmeric
1 teaspoon salt
1 teaspoon coriander powder
1 teaspoon black pepper
5 ozs ghee ($\frac{1}{2}$ teacup)

Wash the lady's fingers and dry with a cloth. Remove both ends and slit lengthwise. Mix amchoor, turmeric, salt, coriander and black pepper together and stuff into lady's fingers. Heat the ghee, fry on low fire until light brown and tender. Serve hot at dinner or lunch.

METHI PANEER
(Serves 6)

½ lb methi (fenugreek leaves) (240 grams)
8 ozs ghee (240 grams)
1 lb paneer
½ teaspoon red chilli powder
¼ teaspoon black pepper
¼ teaspoon turmeric
1 teaspoon ground spices
1 teaspoon coriander powder
½ teaspoon cumin powder
Salt to taste.

Cut the paneer into small cubes and fry in ghee till golden brown. Keep aside. Clean and wash methi leaves. Boil in salted water, drain and grind finely. Heat the ghee, fry ground methi with turmeric until it leaves the ghee. Add the fried paneer, red chilli powder, salt, ground spices, black pepper, coriander and white cumin powders and two teacups water. Cook on low fire till tender and almost dry. Serve hot at lunch or dinner.

DAHIWALE ALOO
(Serves 6)

1 lb medium potatoes (½ kg)
8 ozs curds (250 grams)
1 teaspoon white cumin powder
1 teaspoon turmeric
1 teaspoon chopped coriander leaves
1 teaspoon chopped green chillies
2 teaspoons ground spices
Salt to taste
½ teaspoon red chilli powder
5 ozs ghee (½ teacup)

Deep fry the peeled whole potatoes in ghee, on a low fire, until light brown. Remove from the ghee. Heat 5 ozs ghee, add cumin powder and fry for one minute. Add turmeric, red chilli powder and curd and stir until light brown. Add the fried potatoes, salt and 1½ to 2 teacups water and cook on a low fire until potatoes are tender. Mix chopped coriander, green chillies, and spices. Remove from the fire. Serve hot at lunch or dinner.

POTATO CHIPS

Method

Peel and cut 8 ozs potatoes very thin. Soak in water for half an hour. Deep fry in ghee until light brown. Drain. Sprinkle salt on chips. Serve hot.

TINDA BHUJIA
(Serves 6)

1 lb tinda ($\frac{1}{2}$ kg)
2 big onions
3 teaspoons ground fresh ginger
6 garlic cloves
2 teaspoons coriander powder
1 teaspoon white cumin seeds
2 teaspoons ground spices
4 ozs curd (120 grams)
2 green cardamoms
2 tomatoes
1 teaspoon red chilli powder
2 ozs khoya (60 grams)
Salt to taste
2 tablespoons ghee

Peel the tindas and make four cuts in each. Deep fry in ghee until light brown. Fry ground onion, garlic and green cardamoms until brown. Add one cup water, red chilli powder, ginger and stir until onion is tender. Now add ground spices, coriander powder and coarsely ground white cumin. curd, chopped tomatoes and fried tinda and stir until gravy is cooked. Now add the khoya and stir for 2 minutes. Serve hot at dinner or lunch.

STUFFED TOMATOES
(Serves 10)

1½ lbs tomatoes (750 grams)

6 ozs French beans (180 grams)

3 carrots

1 turnip

6 ozs peas (180 grams)

8 ozs potatoes (250 grams)

1½ onions

2 teaspoons fresh ginger pieces

3 to 4 green chillies

4 teaspoons flour

A few coriander leaves

½ teaspoon black pepper

Salt to taste

1½ tablespoons ghee

8 teaspoons tomato ketchup

2 teaspoons cumin powder

Scoop out the pulp from the tomatoes. Steam all chopped vegetables and boil potatoes. Fry the chopped onions, ginger, green chillies until light brown; then add salt, black pepper and flour and fry. Add two tablespoons of tomato pulp, steamed vegetables and small pieces of potatoes and cook for five minutes until dry. Cool it and fill in tomatoes. Heat the ghee in a frying pan, put stuffed tomatoes, cumin seeds and tomato ketchup. Add half teaspoon salt and cook for 3 minutes. Turn the tomatoes and again cook for 2 minutes. Remove from the fire. Serve hot with potato chips.

MASALA ARBI
(Serves 8)

2 lbs arbi (1 kg)
1 teaspoon turmeric
3 teaspoons ground spices
2 teaspoons coriander powder
4 ozs onion (120 grams)
2 teaspoons ground fresh ginger
8 ozs tomatoes (250 grams)
2 teaspoons chopped coriander
Salt to taste
6 ozs ghee (¾ teacup)

Peel, wash and dry the arbi. Cut into big pieces and fry until light brown. Heat the ghee and fry ground onion, ginger, turmeric and red chilli powder until light brown. Add the arbi and fry it with massala until it is nicely browned. Put in peeled and chopped tomatoes and stir till thick and smooth gravy is formed. Mix in ground spices and coriander leaves. Serve hot at lunch or dinner.

BRINJAL BHURTHA
(Serves 4)

1 lb big brinjals ($\frac{1}{2}$ kg)
2 big onions
6 ozs tomatoes (180 grams)
$\frac{1}{2}$ teaspoon black pepper
$\frac{1}{2}$ teaspoon red chilli powder
4 ozs ghee ($\frac{1}{2}$ teacup)
Salt to taste

Grill the whole brinjals over charcoal fire or bake in an oven on a wire rack until tender and skin is burnt. Put in cold water and peel the skin. Mash well. Heat the ghee, fry the chopped onions until light brown and mix in mashed brinjals and chopped tomatoes. Stir until it leaves the sides of the pan. Remove from the fire, mix with black pepper and red chilli powder. Serve hot at lunch or dinner.

CAPSICUM BHUJIA
(Serves 6)

8 ozs capsicums (240 grams)
4 ozs onions (120 grams)
8 ozs tomatoes (240 grams)
¾ teaspoon turmeric
4 ozs ghee (½ cup)
1 teaspoon ground spices
1 teaspoon chopped coriander leaves
Salt to taste

    Cut the onions into slices. Cut the capsicums and tomatoes into big pieces. Heat the ghee, add turmeric, and fry capsicums, onions and tomatoes together with salt, until dry. Add the ground spices and coriander leaves. Serve hot at lunch or dinner.

CAPSICUM AND POTATO BHUJIA
(Serves 6)

1 lb potatoes (½ kg)
8 ozs capsicums (240 grams)
1 teaspoon turmeric
1 teaspoon black pepper
2 teaspoons amchoor
4 ozs ghee
1 teaspoon ground spices
1 teaspoon white cumin seeds
Salt to taste

    Boil the potatoes in salted water until half tender. Heat the ghee, fry cumin seeds, turmeric, small pieces of potatoes and capsicums on a low fire until light brown. Add salt, black pepper, ground spices, amchoor and mix well. Serve at lunch or dinner.

63

CAPSICUMS STUFFED WITH POTATOES
(Serves 6)

8 ozs capsicums (250 grams)
12 ozs boiled potatoes (360 grams)
2 to 3 green chillies
1 teaspoon chopped coriander leaves
2 teaspoons chopped fresh ginger
5 ozs ghee (½ teacup)
½ teaspoon turmeric
½ teaspoon ground spices
1 tablespoon amchoor
Salt to taste

Chop boiled potatoes and green chillies. Heat some ghee, add turmeric and fry the chopped ingredients for a few minutes. Remove from the fire, add salt, ground spices and amchoor and mix well. Slit the capsicums lengthwise, fill with the cooked potatoes and put them in the same pan and cover. Cook on very low fire until tender. Serve hot at lunch or dinner.

CAPSICUMS STUFFED WITH SPICES
(Serves 6)

8 ozs capsicums (250 grams)
½ teaspoon turmeric
3 teaspoons white cumin powder
3 teaspoons coriander powder
2 cloves (ground)
1 tablespoon amchoor
½ teaspoon black pepper
¼ teaspoon ground cinnamon
1 lb curd (½ kg)
Salt to taste
5 ozs ghee (½ teacup)
¼ teaspoon asafoetida water

Heat the ghee, add asafoetida water, turmeric, curd, ground spices, salt and pepper and stir until brown. Remove from the fire, add amchoor and cool. Slit the capsicums lengthwise and fill the fried spices in them. Cover the pan and cook on low heat until capsicums are tender. Serve hot at lunch or dinner.

FRIED CHANA WITH GRAVY
(Serves 8)

1 lb chana ($\frac{1}{2}$ kg)
1 $\frac{1}{2}$ pints water (6 teacups)
1 $\frac{1}{2}$ teaspoons chilli powder
1 tablespoon ghee
4 teaspoons salt for the the masala below
4 teaspoons ground spices
8 level teaspoons amchoor
2 teaspoons white cumin powder
4 ozs tamarind (120 grams)
1 teaspoon chilli powder for tamarind
8 ozs tomatoes (250 grams)
8 green chillies
4 medium onions
2 ozs ginger slices (60 grams)

Soak the chana overnight. Heat the ghee, put red chilli powder and soaked chana and boil in the same water until tender. Add amchoor, spices and cumin powder and mix lightly. Slice the onions and chop tomatoes. Cut ginger into long strips. Soak the tamarind in 1$\frac{1}{2}$ cups water, pass it through a sieve and mix it with red chilli powder. Serve onions, tomatoes, green chillies and tamarind pulp separately. Serve hot at lunch with plain puris.

LADY'S FINGERS IN TOMATO SAUCE
(Serves 6)

1 lb lady's fingers ($\frac{1}{2}$ kg)
1 lb tomatoes ($\frac{1}{2}$ kg)
1 teaspoon chopped ginger
1 spring onion
$\frac{1}{4}$ teaspoon red chilli powder
Salt to taste
2 cloves
6 peppercorns
6 ozs ghee ($\frac{3}{4}$ teacup)

Wash and dry the lady's fingers. Fry them whole with a little salt in ghee until light brown and tender. Remove from the ghee. Chop the spring onion and tomatoes. Cook the chopped ingredients, salt, cloves, peppercorns and red chilli powder together in a pan or degchi until tender. Pass through a sieve. Heat it and mix fried lady's fingers with it and stir for a few minutes. Serve hot at lunch or dinner.

DUM ALOO
(Serves 8)

1 ½ lbs medium potatoes (¾ kg)
4 ozs ghee (½ teacup)
1 teaspoon red chilli powder (Kashmiri mirch)
A few drops of asafoetida water
1 ½ teaspoons withe cumin powder
4 dessertspoons curd
1 teaspoon ground spices
½ teaspoon ground fresh ginger
Salt to taste
A few coriander leaves

Boil the potatoes in salt water. Peel and prick them with a toothpick. Deep fry in ghee on a low fire until brown. Melt the ghee in a degchi and put the curd, cumin powder and asafoetida water in it. When the curd becomes golden brown add some water. When gravy is a little thick add the potatoes. Sprinkle coriander leaves, ground spices and cover the degchi. Simmer for a few minutes. Serve hot at lunch or dinner.

6

D A L

SPECIAL FRIED URAD DAL
(Serves 6)

2 cups urad dal
5 cups water
2 teaspoons turmeric
1 teaspoon black pepper
1 teaspoon black cumin seeds
2 medium tomatoes
1 oz ginger (30 grams)
½ or ¾ cup butter ghee
1 big onion
2 teaspoons chopped coriander leaves
2 green chillies
Salt to taste

Wash and soak the dal for 15 minutes. Fry chopped onion and ginger in butter ghee until light brown, add cumin seeds and fry for one minute. Add the chopped tomatoes and stir for one minute. Boil water, add dal, turmeric and salt and cook on low fire. When dal is nearly cooked, add fried onion, ginger, cumin seeds, tomatoes, chopped coriander leaves, green chillies and black pepper and cook for 5 minutes.

MUGLAI DAL
(Serves 6)

1½ teacups urad dal (without husk)
3½ cups water
1 level teaspoon turmeric
4 ozs paneer (120 grams)
1 level teaspoon black pepper
4 green chillies
Few coriander leaves
¾ level teaspoon black cumin seeds
2 teaspoons chopped ginger
1 small onion
1 medium firm tomato
2 ozs ghee (¼ teacup)
Salt to taste
¼ cup cream

Soak the urad dal for one hour. Boil water with turmeric and salt. Add soaked urad dal, fried paneer and cook till the dal becomes tender and each grain is separate. Strain, so that excess water may trickle down. Now fry finely chopped onion in ghee till slightly golden. Add finely chopped ginger, and fry till onion is golden brown. Add black cumin seeds and fry a little and mix into the dal. Also mix chopped green chillies and coriander leaves.

At the time of serving put the dal in a dish and sprinkle chopped tomato without pulp and pour the cream over it.

PANCH RATNI DAL
(Serves 6)

2 ozs chana dal (60 grams)
2 ozs whole moong dal (60 grams)
2 ozs whole urad dal (60 grams)
2 ozs whole masoor dal (60 grams)
1 oz arhar dal (30 grams)
1 teaspoon turmeric
2 teaspoons ground fresh ginger
A tiny piece of asafoetida
4 ozs ghee ($\frac{1}{2}$ teacup)
$\frac{1}{2}$ teaspoon red chilli powder
$\frac{1}{2}$ teaspoon black pepper
1 teaspoon black cumin seeds
1 big tomato
1 small onion
1 teaspoon chopped green chillies
1 tablespoon curd
3 tablespoons ghee
Salt to taste

Pick and wash the dals. Boil enough water and add the dals and turmeric and cook until the dals are half tender. Heat 1 oz ghee and fry asafoetida until light brown and crush it. Mix it with half cooked dals with some ghee, salt and curd and cook until the dals are tender and well mixed. Add red chilli powder and black pepper. Heat the ghee, fry chopped onion and ginger until light brown, add black cumin seeds, chopped green chillies, chopped tomatoes without pulp and stir them for a few minutes. Now mix them with the dal. Serve hot at dinner or lunch. (This dal takes 4 hours to cook.)

RASAM (SOUTH INDIAN)
(Serves 6)

4 ozs arhar dal (120 grams)

2 ozs tamarind (60 grams)

25 ozs water (5 teacups)

1 teaspoon turmeric

1½ teaspoons red chilli powder

4 drops asafoetida water

3 teaspoons mustard powder

2 tomatoes

2 tablespoons ghee

4 green chillies

2 teaspoons jaggery

3 tablespoons coriander seeds

4 whole red chillies

2 ozs fresh coconut (60 grams)

10 black peppercorns

Salt to taste

Pick and wash the dal and cook in water until tender. Pass through a sieve. Soak tamarind in a cup of water for 10 minutes, and pass through a sieve. Grind coriander seeds, 4 red chillies, coconut and black peppercorns finely with a little water. Mix all the ingredients with mashed dal, ghee, and coriander leaves and cook until a little thick. Remove from the fire. Splutter mustard seeds in ghee and mix with rasam. Sprinkle chopped coriander leaves. Serve hot at lunch or dinner with boiled rice.

SHAHI DAL

(Serves 6)

8 ozs urad dal (250 grams)
12 ozs milk (2½ teacups)
5 ozs water (1 cup)
4 green cardamoms
1 tomato without pulp
8 blanched almonds (slit into halves)
¼ teaspoon black pepper
½ teaspoon turmeric
½ teaspoon red chilli powder
2 teaspoon chopped coriander leaves
1 teaspoon chopped ginger
1 small onion
5 oz ghee (½ teacup)
½ teaspoon black cumin seeds
Salt to taste

Pick and wash the dal. Put dal in a mixture of milk and water, with 3 ozs ghee, turmeric, red chilli powder, cardamoms, salt and almonds. Cook on low fire until tender and water-milk mixture are absorbed and each grain is separate. Heat the ghee, fry chopped onion and ginger until light brown. Then add black cumin seeds, chopped tomato without pulp and coriander leaves and stir for one minute. Mix with cooked dal and sprinkle black pepper. Serve at lunch or dinner.

SPECIAL MIXED DAL
(Serves 6)

2 ozs moong dal without husk (60 grams)

2 ozs urad dal without husk (60 grams)

2 ozs chana dal (60 grams)

2 ozs whole masoor (60 grams)

$3\frac{1}{4}$ pints water (12 teacups)

2 teaspoons ground spices

1 teaspoon turmeric

A tiny piece of asafoetida

5 ozs ghee ($\frac{1}{2}$ teacup)

1 big onion

2 teaspoons chopped fresh ginger

1 teaspoon white cumin seeds

1 teaspoon black cumin seeds

$\frac{1}{2}$ teaspoon red chilli powder

$\frac{1}{2}$ teaspoon black pepper

Salt to taste

1 bay leaf

4 ozs curd (120 grams)

2 whole red chillies

Pick, wash and soak all the dals overnight. Boil water, add the dals, white cumin seeds, salt, asafoetida and ginger and cook until tender. Add the curd, red chilli powder and black pepper and cook until well mixed. Heat the ghee, fry bay leaf, whole red chillies and chopped onion until light brown. Add black cumin seeds and stir for a minute. Mix with dal and cook for a few minutes. Sprinkle with ground spices. Serve hot at lunch or dinner with chapatis and boiled rice.

SABUT URAD DAL
(Serves 12)

1 lb whole urad dal ($\frac{1}{2}$ kg)
3$\frac{1}{4}$ pints water (12 teacups)
1 teaspoon black pepper
A little asafoetida
6 cloves garlic
1 onion
1 teaspoon black cumin seeds
2 tablespoons ghee
2 teaspoons chopped ginger
Salt to taste

Pick and wash the urad dal. Boil water, add urad dal and cook on a low fire until half cooked. Add asafoetida, black pepper, chopped garlic, ginger and onion and cook until tender and well mixed. Heat the ghee, fry black cumin seeds for one minute and mix with dal. Serve at dinner or lunch.

7

RAITA

BRINJAL RAITA
(Serves 6)

1 big brinjal (12 ozs or 360 grams)
1 lb curd ($\frac{1}{2}$ kg)
1 teaspoon chopped mint leaves
$\frac{1}{2}$ teaspoon black cumin seeds
$\frac{1}{2}$ teaspoon black pepper
$\frac{1}{2}$ teaspoon red chilli powder
Salt to taste

Grill whole brinjal over charcoal fire or bake in an oven on a wire rack and baste it frequently until tender and the skin is burnt. Put into cold water, remove the skin, and mash i t. Beat the curd with salt, red chilli powder, black pepper and cumin seeds and then mix in mashed brinjal and mint leaves. Serve cold at lunch or dinner. (If raita is thick, add 3 to 4 tablespoons water and mix well.)

DAHI BARA
(Serves 10)

12 ozs whole urad dal (360 grams)
1 teaspoon chopped coriander
2 green chillies (chopped)
1 teaspoon ground spices
½ teaspoon black cumin seeds
¼ teaspoon soda bicarbonate
Ghee for deep frying
2 lbs curd (1 kg)
Salt for curd
Mint leaves

Soak the urad dal overnight, then remove the husk. Grind finely and mix chopped green chillies, coriander, ground spices, chilli powder and soda bicarbonate with it and beat until light. Wet the palm of your hand with a little water, put some mixture on it and form into a round and flat ball, then gently drop it in hot ghee. Fry it until evenly browned on both sides. Drain well, and then immerse in cold water. Beat the curd with salt, 1 teaspoon black pepper, ¼ teaspoon red chilli powder and 1 teaspoon black cumin seeds. If the curd is too thick add a few tablespoons of water. Squeeze out the water carefully from the 'bara' (Press them between the palms of your hands without breaking), and put them in the curd. Sprinkle with chopped mint leaves and ¼ teaspoon red chilli powder. Serve cold at lunch or dinner. (Several balls or baras can be fried simultaneously).

PAKORI RAITA
(Serves 6)

1 lb curd ($\frac{1}{2}$ kg)
$\frac{1}{2}$ teaspoon black cumin seeds
Salt to taste
1 teaspoon chopped mint leaves
$\frac{1}{2}$ teaspoon black pepper
$\frac{1}{2}$ teaspoon red chilli powder
4 to 5 ozs besan (120 or 150 grams)
Ghee for frying

Make a batter of besan with water, of a thick and dropping consistency. Heat the ghee in a deep pan, pour the batter through a big-holed skimmer and press lightly with hand over the deep pan so that the drops fall into the ghee. Fry in ghee for 2 minutes. When they become crisp, remove; drop into cold water. Beat the curd with salt, pepper, red chilli powder and black cumin seeds. Squeeze out the water carefully from the ɪkories (press them between the palms of your hands without ɪreaking). Put into the curd and decorate with $\frac{1}{4}$ teaspoon red chilli powder and mint leaves. Serve at lunch or dinner.

PUMPKIN (GHIA) RAITA
(Serves 6)

8 ozs pumpkin (250 grams)
1 lb curd ($\frac{1}{2}$ kg)
2 green chillies
$\frac{1}{2}$ teaspoon black pepper
$\frac{1}{4}$ teaspoon red chilli powder
Salt to taste
$\frac{1}{2}$ teaspoon black cumin seeds
2 teaspoons chopped mint leaves

Peel and grate the pumpkin. Boil in water until tender and remove from the fire. Drain and cool. Beat the curd, mix in salt, pepper, cumin seeds, chopped green chillies, mint leaves, and boiled pumpkin. Serve cold at dinner or lunch.

MINT (PUDINA) RAITA
(Serves 6)

1 lb curd (½ kg)
1 tablespoon ground mint leaves
1 teaspoon ground green chillies
½ teaspoon black pepper
Salt to taste

Beat the curd and mix in ground green chillies, ground mint leaves, salt and black pepper. Serve cold at lunch or dinner.

ONION RAITA
(Serves 6)

1 lb curd (½ kg)
4 ozs onion
2 green chillies
1 teaspoon chopped mint leaves
Salt to taste
1 teaspoon black cumin seeds
½ teaspoon black pepper
½ teaspoon red chilli powder

Cut onion into slices; rub with 1 teaspoon salt and keep for 10 minutes and wash them well. Beat the curd with salt, pepper, red chilli powder, cumin seeds and chopped green chillies and then mix onion slices and chopped mint leaves in it. Serve cold at lunch or dinner.

8

S N A C K S

ENERGY KABAB
(Serves 8)

1 turnip

4 ozs peas (120 grams)

2 carrots

4 ozs beans (120 grams)

1 boiled potato

2 green chillies

¼ teaspoon black pepper

½ small onion

1 teaspoon chopped coriander leaves

3 teaspoons dry breadcrumbs

¼ teaspoon red chilli powder

5 to 6 teaspoons flour

1½ teaspoon chopped ginger

Ghee for frying

3 teaspoons ghee

1 oz flour for making batter (30 grams)

4 teaspoons whipped cream

¼ oz grated cheese (7 grams)

2½ ozs butter (75 grams)

81

4 ozs potatoes (120 grams)
Salt to taste

Chop all the vegetables and steam them until tender. Fry chopped onion, green chillies and ginger in ½ oz ghee until light brown. Add the flour and fry for one minute then put in steamed vegetables, salt and pepper. Cook for 2 minutes. Chill and add 3 teaspoons dry breadcrumbs and mix well. Make a paste of butter, grated cheese, whipped cream and chill. Make balls of the chilled paste and cover with the vegetable mixture and shape into round balls. Dust with flour and dip into 1 oz flour batter and roll in breadcrumbs. Deep fry in ghee until brown. Drain on paper. Put the energy kababs on 4 ozs boiled and mashed potatoes and serve hot.

SEEKH KABAB (VEGETARIAN)
(Serves 8)

1½ lbs bhein or kamal kakri (750 grams)
½ onion
1 teaspoon ground ginger
3 green chillies
3 teaspoons white cumin powder
2 teaspoons ground spices
2 teaspoons chopped coriander leaves
2 to 3 ozs roasted and ground chana
Salt to taste
¼ teaspoon red chilli powder
1 tablespoon ghee

Scrape and cut bhein into thin slices and boil in salted water until tender. Remove from the fire, cool and mash. Add salt, ground spices, ginger, white cumin powder, chopped coriander leaves, onion, green chillies, red chilli powder and ground chana and mix well. Put the mixture on skewers and grill on a charcoal fire or in an oven until light brown. Heat one tablespoon ghee in a frying pan, and fry seekh kababs until brown. Serve with tomato ketchup at dinner or lunch.

83

POTATO KABAB (PARSI)
(Serves 10)

1½ lbs potatoes (725 grams)
1 teaspoon salt for boiling potatoes
½ fresh coconut or one teacup of grated dry coconut
2 teaspoons chopped coriander leaves
2 slices bread
3 green chillies
½ teaspoon red chilli powder
2 teaspoons ground spices
1 teaspoon white cumin seeds
2 teaspoons finely chopped ginger
1 medium tomato
1 oz flour for batter (30 grams)
Ghee for deep frying
Dry breadcrumbs for coating
Salt to taste

Boil the potatoes in salted water until tender. Cool and mash. Scrape the brown part of the fresh coconut and grate. If using dry grated coconut, soak in one teacup water for 35 minutes and then squeeze it through a thin cloth. Soak the bread in water and squeeze. Heat one tablespoon ghee and fry chopped ginger, green chillies and grated coconut until light brown. Add chopped coriander leaves, ground spices, ground white cumin seeds, salt, chopped tomatoes, soaked bread slices, red chilli powder and cook until the mixture is dry. Cool the mixture. Make 12 round balls of mashed potatoes and fill them with cooked coconut mixture. Make a batter of flour and dip the kababs into it. Roll in dry breadcrumbs. Fry in hot ghee until light brown. Drain on paper and serve at tea or breakfast.

RICE KABAB
(Serves 8)

4 ozs rice flour (120 grams)

1 pint milk (4 teacups)

2 ozs butter (60 grams)

1 oz flour for batter

2 ozs cheese

1½ cups breadcrumbs

1 teaspoon cumin powder

½ teaspoon red chilli powder

¼ teaspoon black pepper

1 ground clove

1 chopped green chilli

1 teaspoon chopped coriander leaves

Slices of one lemon

A few mint leaves

Salt to taste

Boil the milk with butter, add rice flour and stir until thick. Remove from the fire, add grated cheese, salt, pepper, red chilli powder, chopped green chillies, clove, cumin powder and coriander leaves. Chill, then make into oblong shapes. Dip in flour batter and coat with breadcrumbs. Deep fry in ghee until brown. Decorate with lemon slices and mint leaves. Serve with tomato sauce at breakfast.

FRUIT CHAT
(Serves 8)

Masala
3 teaspoons ground spices
2 teaspoons black pepper powder
3 teaspoons red chilli powder
1½ teaspoons salt
3 teaspoons amchoor
1½ teaspoons black salt
¼ teaspoon citric acid
2 teaspoons fine sugar
7 teaspoons cumin seeds
1 teaspoon thymol powder

Mix all the above ground spices together except cumin seeds. Roast cumin seeds on a griddle till light brown and grind.

Fruits
8 ozs potatoes (250 grams)
8 lemons (250 grams)
1 kachalu
8 ozs peas (250 grams)
8 sweet potatoes (shakarkandi, 240 grams)
8 ozs guava (250 grams)
8 ozs papaya (250 grams)
4 bananas
1 tomato without pulp
1 teaspoon salt for boiling peas and potatoes

Boil sweet potatoes, peas and potatoes together in salted water till tender. Boil the kachalu also in salted water, but separately. Cut all the fruits into small pieces. Add masala and lemon juice and mix well. Sprinkle the cumin powder over it.

PANEER PAKORAS
(Serves 8)

6 ozs besan (1½ teacups)

8 ozs paneer (240 grams)

⅛ teaspoon baking powder

¼ teaspoon thymol seeds

½ teaspoon red chilli powder

Salt to taste

Ghee for deep frying

Make a thick batter of besan with water, salt, ground thymol seeds, red chilli powder and baking powder. Cut paneer into big and thin pieces and rub a little salt into them. Dip paneer pieces into the batter. Fry in hot ghee till golden brown and crisp. Serve immediately at tea.

RUSSIAN SANDWICHES
(Serves 12)

2½ ozs butter (8 teaspoons)

1 tin (1 lb) cream cheese

1 teaspoon red chilli sauce

½ teaspoon salt

1½ tablespoons tomato ketchup

1 teaspoon mustard powder

3 ozs cheese (½ teacup)

2 lbs bread (1 kg)

Mix butter, cream cheese, salt, chilli sauce and mustard powder to a soft paste. Grate the cheese. Cut the bread lengthwise into ¼ inch thick slices. Remove the hard crusts. Spread the soft paste with a flat knife and then the grated cheese and roll tightly. Wrap each roll in butter paper, fix with toothpicks and chill. When ready to serve cut into ¼ inch thick slices. Serve at tea.

VEGETABLE SAMOSA
(Serves 12)

Filling

1 lb potatoes (½ kg)

4 teaspoons coarse coriander powder

3 teaspoons white cumin seeds

1 teaspoon red chilli powder

1 teaspoon black pepper

3 green chillies

1 teaspoon chopped coriander leaves

2 ozs boiled peas (60 grams)

1 tablespoon ghee

Salt to taste

Boil the potatoes, peel and cut into small pieces. Heat the ghee, add potatoes, spices, chopped coriander leaves, peas, green chillies and salt and cook for two minutes. Cool and keep aside.

Covering

1 lb flour (½ kg)

7 or 8 tablespoons melted ghee

1 level teaspoon salt

7 to 8 tablespoons water

Sift the flour with salt. Mix ghee and water into it. Rub with fingertips and knead it with water. Make 2 dozen balls. Roll out each ball into a thin round, 4″ in diameter and then cut into half. Wet the edges of one half and place one side over the other to form a cone. Fill the cooked potato mixture in it andpressthe edges together. Deep fry in ghee until light brown. Drain and serve hot at tea.

POTATO BONDA (SOUTH INDIAN)
(Serves 8)

1 lb potatoes ($\frac{1}{2}$ kg)
2 ozs onions ($\frac{3}{4}$ teacup)
3 green chillies
1 teaspoon chopped coriander leaves
1 teaspoon chopped fresh ginger
$\frac{1}{4}$ teaspoon turmeric
$\frac{1}{4}$ teaspoon mustard seeds
1 oz ghee (3 teaspoons)
8 ozs besan (2 teacups)
Salt to taste
Oil for deep frying
$1\frac{1}{2}$ teacups water for the besan batter

Boil the potatoes. Cool, peel and chop them. Chop the
onions and green chillies. Heat the ghee, and fry onions, ginger,
green chillies with salt, turmeric and mustard seeds for one
minute. Add the potatoes and stir for a few minutes. Remove
from the fire. Mix with chopped coriander leaves and cool. Take
sufficient potato mixture to form a ball, the size of a billiard
ball. Make the batter with besan and water to a thick dropping
consistency. Mix in a little salt. Dip the potato balls into it and
fry in very hot oil until golden brown. Serve hot at tea.

CLUB SANDWICHES

(Serves 8)

12 slices bread

4 ozs butter

½ teaspoon mustard powder

¼ teaspoon white pepper

½ teaspoon salt

5 gherkins

4 ozs cashewnuts (¾ teacup)

6 pickled onions

6 tomatoes

8 ozs potatoes for wafers (250 grams)

2 medium cucumbers

1 tablespoon cream

3 cheese slices

Cream the butter, add cream, mustard powder, chopped gherkins, sliced pickled onions and mix well. Brown the bread on one side and spread the butter mixture on the other side. Cover with another slice of bread. On top of this place a cheese slice and over it a bread slice. Put tomato slices on it and cover it with a slice of bread. Spread cucumber slices on it and place a buttered slice to cover. Press well together. Fasten it with 4 toothpicks and then cut into 4 triangles. Put them on a plate and decorate with fried cashewnuts and potato wafers. Serve at tea. (Fry cashewnuts in hot ghee till light brown. Drain on paper and sprinkle salt.)

ALMOND KABAB
(Serves 8)

4 ozs blanched almonds (120 grams)
3½ ozs fresh breadcrumbs (100 grams)
8 ozs milk (1¾ cup)
1½ ozs butter (45 grams)
1½ ozs flour (45 grams)
1 small onion
2 teaspoons chopped coriander leaves
4 green chillies
Salt to taste
1 teaspoon cumin powder
2 teaspoons chopped mint leaves
¼ teaspoon red chilli powder
Dry breadcrumbs for coating
1 oz flour for batter (30 grams)
Ghee for deep frying

Grind blanched almonds finely. Fry the chopped onion and green chillies until light brown. Boil the milk with butter and add sifted flour and stir it over the fire until it leaves the sides and bottom of the degchi. Add the almond paste, fried onion and green chillies, fresh breadcrumbs, cumin powder, salt, coriander leaves and red chilli powder and mix. Remove from the fire, spread it on a plate and chill. Make into oblong shapes, dip into a thin flour batter and roll in breadcrumbs. Deep fry until nicely browned. Drain on paper. Sprinkle with chopped mint leaves and serve hot with tomato ketchup. (Flour batter should be thinad smooth).

DAL KABAB

(Serves 8)

8 ozs chana dal (250 grams)
1½ lbs boiled potatoes (½ kg)
1 tablespoon milk
1 teaspoon chopped ginger
1 teaspoon chopped coriander leaves
1 teaspoon chopped onion
2 teaspoons chopped green chillies
¼ teaspoon black pepper
¼ teaspoon red chilli powder
2 teaspoons ground spices
1 oz flour for batter (30 grams)
Breadcrumbs for coating
Ghee for frying

Pick, wash the chana dal and boil it in salt water until tender. Put in a strainer to remove excess water. Grate the boiled potatoes, mix with milk, salt and black pepper. Mix chopped ingredients, salt and red chilli powder with boiled dal. Take some of the potato mixture and flatten it out. Make a cup-shaped depression in the centre, and fill it with the dal mixture. Now cover with more of the potato mixture. Flatten and shape into round cakes each 2 inches in diameter. Dip into flour batter and roll in breadcrumbs. Fry in hot ghee until golden brown. Drain on paper. Serve hot at breakfast or tea with mint chutney or tomato ketchup.

MIXED VEGETABLE CREAM KABAB
(Serves 8)

2 turnips
8 ozs peas (250 grams)
4 carrots
8 ozs beans (250 grams)
2 boiled potatoes
4 green chillies
½ teaspoon black pepper
2 teaspoons cumin powder
1 small onion
2 teaspoons chopped coriander leaves
2 tablespoons dry breadcrumbs
½ teaspoon red chilli powder
8 teaspoons flour
1 teaspoon chopped ginger
2 ozs butter (60 grams)
2 ozs cream (¼ teacup)
Breadcrumbs for coating
2 ozs flour for batter
Ghee for frying
Salt to taste

Chop all the vegetables and steam or boil them. Fry the chopped onion, green chillies and ginger in ½ oz of ghee until light brown. Add the flour and fry for one minute. Add steamed vegetables, salt, pepper, red chilli powder and cumin powder and cook for 3 minutes. Chill, add 2 tablespoons breadcrumbs and mix well. Make a paste of the whipped cream and butter and chill it. Make oval shaped cutlets and fill chilled cream in each. Dust with flour, dip into flour batter and roll in breadcrumbs. Deep fry in ghee until brown. Drain on paper and serve with tomato ketchup.

SEMOLINA KABAB
(Serves 8)

4 ozs semolina (125 grams)
¾ pint milk (3 teacups)
2 ozs butter (60 grams)
3 ozs grated cheese (90 grams)
½ teaspoon red chilli powder
2 or 3 green chillies
A few green coriander leaves
A few mint leaves
3 teaspoons tomato ketchup
2 teaspoons chopped ginger
1 teaspoon ground spices
Salt to taste
Ghee for frying
Breadcrumbs for coating
2 ozs flour for batter (60 grams)

Heat the milk with butter and add semolina. Cook until the
mixture is thick. Remove from the fire. Add grated cheese, salt,
red chilli powder, ground coriander and mint leaves, green chillies,
ginger, tomato ketchup and ground spices. Spread this mixture
on a plate and chill until set. Cut into cutlet shapes. Dust with
flour, dip into flour batter and roll in breadcrumbs. Deep fry in
ghee until brown. Serve with tomato ketchup at breakfast or
tea.

BREAD KABAB

(Serves 8)

8 bread slices

$\frac{1}{2}$ cup milk

$\frac{1}{4}$ teaspoon ground nutmeg

$\frac{1}{2}$ teaspoon white pepper

2 teaspoons chopped coriander leaves

Rind of 1 lemon

1 egg

$\frac{1}{4}$ teaspoon ground spices

1 to 1$\frac{1}{2}$ cups dry breadcrumbs

Ghee for frying

Salt to taste

Cut the slices of bread into rectangular shapes, $\frac{3}{4}$" thick. Pour the milk into a plate and dip the slices in it. Mix together the coriander leaves, ground spices, lemon rind, salt, pepper and nutmeg and sprinkle on the slices. Beat the egg lightly with $\frac{1}{4}$ cup water, dip the slices into it and then roll in the breadcrumbs. Fry in hot ghee till golden brown. Drain on paper and serve hot at tea.

COCKTAIL FISH KABAB
(Serves 8)

12 ozs fish (360 grams)

3 ozs chana dal (90 grams)

3 teacups water

1 small onion

4 small pieces ginger

2 cloves

1½ teaspoons white cumin seeds

2 green chillies

1" piece cinnamon

1 or 2 egg yolks

2 teaspoons chopped coriander leaves

6 cloves garlic

¼ teaspoon red chilli powder

Salt to taste

Ghee for frying

Wash and soak the chana dal for 15 minutes. Cook in the same water with cloves, cinnamon, cumin seeds and garlic until nearly tender. Drain and retain its water for boiling the fish. Boil the fish until tender and the water is absorbed. Cool, remove the bones and skin and then grind it with chana dal. Grind onion, green chillies, ginger and coriander leaves finely and mix with the mixture of fish and dal. Mix in the egg yolks and form into small round balls. Deep fry in ghee until brown. Drain on paper. Insert a toothpick in each kabab and serve hot.

KASHMIRI KABAB
(Serves 6)

8 ozs minced meat (240 grams)
1 teaspoon chopped ginger
1 teaspoon cumin seeds
2 cloves
1 big cardamom
1 small piece cinnamon
1½ cups milk
2 green chillies
2 teaspoons chopped coriander leaves
1 egg white
4 garlic flakes
Salt to taste
Ghee for deep frying

Cook all the above ingredients together except the egg white, till tender and dry. Cool and grind it finely. Make oblong balls and dip in egg white and fry till golden brown. Serve at tea with mint chutney.

SHIKAM PURI KABAB
(Serves 6)

1 lb minced lean meat ($\frac{1}{2}$ kg)

1 onion

4 garlic cloves

2″ piece ginger

3 green chillies

4 teaspoons chopped green coriander leaves

4 almonds

1 teaspoon cheronjee

A very small piece cinnamon

2 cardamoms

3 cloves

1 teaspoon cumin seeds

1 tablespoonful besan

2 ozs fresh coconut (60 grams)

2 ozs curd (60 grams)

Mint leaves

Salt to taste

1$\frac{1}{2}$ cups dry breadcrumbs

1 or 2 eggs

Ghee for frying

Chop onion, garlic, ginger and chillies very finely and fry in ghee until light brown. Grind the green coriander leaves, almonds, cheronjee, cinnamon, cardamoms and cloves and mix with besan. Fry the onion, garlic and ginger till golden in colour and mix besan mixture in it. Then add minced meat, salt and one tablespoonful of coconut milk and cook until the water of the meat is absorbed. Turn out the contents and grind this mixture into a fine paste. Strain the curd through a coarse cloth. Blend together strained curd and ground fresh mint with a pinch of salt. Take sufficient meat paste to form a ball, the size of a billiard ball, and make a hollow in the

98

centre in which place a little curd mixture. Then gradually work the meat upwards until the curd is covered completely and a round flat cutlet is formed. Roll the cutlet in breadcrumbs. Fry golden brown in hot ghee.

To prepare coconut milk, grind coconut finely, add 1½ tablespoons water and mix well. Strain through a muslin cloth and use in kababs.

KABAB STUFFED WITH MEAT
(Serves 6)

1 lb potatoes (½ kg)
½ oz butter (15 grams)
1 oz milk (⅛ teacup)
½ teaspoon red chilli powder
Dry breadcrumbs
1 egg
Salt to taste
Ghee for frying

Boil and mash the potatoes, add butter, milk, salt and red chilli powder and mix. Cook for 3 minutes. Remove from the fire and cool. Take sufficient potato paste and make into a square shape. Fill in it cooked minced meat and shape it triangular. Beat the egg with a little water. Using a little flour on the kababs dip into the beaten egg and roll in dry breadcrumbs. Deep fry till golden brown in ghee. Serve hot with curd chutney.

Filling

4 ozs minced meat (120 grams)
1 medium chopped onion
3 slices ginger
2 green chillies

2 teaspoons chopped coriander leaves

¼ teaspoon red chilli powder

¼ teaspoon turmeric

1 tablespoon ghee

½ small tomato

1 teaspoon flour

Salt to taste

Fry the chopped onion and ginger golden brown. Add chopped tomato, green chillies, coriander leaves, turmeric and a little water and stir for 2 minutes. Add minced meat, salt, red chilli powder and ½ cup of water. Cook until tender and dry. Mix in one teaspoon flour and cook for two minutes. Remove from the fire, cool and fill in the kababs.

PORK SEEKH KABAB
(Serves 6)

1 lb minced pork leg meat with very little fat (½ kg)

2 small onions

2 green chillies

½ teaspoon red chilli powder

6 teaspoons coarse cumin powder

3 garlic cloves

2 teaspoons ground spices

2 small eggs

4 teaspoons chopped coriander leaves

Chop the onions, green chillies and coriander. Wash and dry with a duster. Grind the garlic finely. Mix the chopped ingredients, ground garlic, spices, chillies and yolk of eggs with minced pork. Pack it tightly on iron skewers and grill on the fire till light brown. If the mixture is soft, add roasted chana flour. Sufficient for 10 persons (22 seekh kababs). Serve at tea or dinner with mint chutney.

CHICKEN TIKKA
(Serves 6)

1 medium chicken
14 garlic cloves
4 big pieces ginger
1 teacup curd
1 teaspoon red chilli powder
6 green cardamoms
1″ piece cinnamon
1 piece mace
½ teaspoon saffron
Salt to taste
3 ozs ghee (¼ teacup)

Grind green cardamoms, cinnamon, mace, and garlic finely. Grind ginger separately with 3 tablespoons of water and strain. Mix the above paste and ginger water with the curd. Clean, wash and dry the chicken. Cut it into small pieces and marinate in the curd mixture for two hours. Put pieces of chicken on the skewers, leaving the ends free. Roast in a tandoor or on a wire rack in a moderate oven until dry and tender. Baste the pieces frequently with ghee. Serve hot with lemon slices at dinner.

FISH TIKKA
(Serves 6)

1 lb sole fish or mackerel (500 grams)
15 garlic cloves
3 small pieces ginger
$\frac{1}{4}$ teaspoon cinnamon powder
1 small piece mace
3 to 4 teaspoons curd
$\frac{1}{2}$ teaspoon orange colour
1$\frac{1}{2}$ teaspoons red chilli powder
Salt to taste

Wash the fish, remove bones and dry with a cloth. Cut into medium pieces. Grind garlic and ginger finely. Grind all the spices. Mix all the ground ingredients, colour, salt, and red chilli powder with curd. Rub into the fish pieces and keep for one hour. Put on the skewers and roast on medium charcoal fire or on a grill, turning frequently till nicely browned. Serve with mint chutney at tea.

CHICKEN TOAST (FRENCH)
(Serves 8)

2 chicken breasts
2 cups milk
4 teaspoons flour
2 teaspoons lemon juice
$\frac{1}{4}$ teaspoon white pepper
$\frac{1}{2}$ teaspoon Worcestershire sauce
8 bread slices
5 teaspoons butter
1 firm tomato
Coriander leaves
Salt to taste

Boil the chicken with $\frac{1}{2}$ teaspoon salt in water till tender. Remove the bones and chop. Fry the flour in butter till golden in colour, add milk and cook till a little thick. Remove from the fire, mix chicken pieces, white pepper, salt, lemon juice and sauce. Put it on buttered toasts and decorate with chopped coriander leaves and firm tomato pieces without pulp. Serve at breakfast.

CHICKEN OMELET SOUFFLE
(Serves 2)

2 eggs
3 teaspoons ghee
1 chicken breast (boiled and chopped)
1 teaspoon coriander leaves
1 green chilli (chopped)
¼ teaspoon white pepper
Salt to taste

Separate the yolks from the whites of eggs. Beat the yolks, white pepper and salt. Whip the whites till stiff and fold lightly into the yolks. Mix in green chilli, coriander leaves and the chopped chicken. Melt the ghee in a frying pan, pour the egg mixture in it and stir on the surface until it begins to set. Sprinkle the chicken pieces on the omelet. Leave until nicely browned underneath. Slip a knife under it and fold first from one side and then from the other towards the centre. Serve at breakfast.

SPECIAL MASALA

3 teaspoons cumin powder
2 teaspoons salt
1 teaspoon black pepper
1 teaspoon red chilli powder
4 teaspoons amchoor

Mix all the above ground spices. Keep in an airtight glass jar and sprinkle on pakoras before serving.

EGG PAKORA
(Serves 8)

6 hard boiled eggs
6 teaspoons special masala

Cut each egg into 4 pieces lengthwise. Rub in the special masala. Dip in pakora batter and fry till golden brown and crisp. Serve with mint chutney at tea.
(Pakora batter in this case is prepared in the usual way).

FRIED FISH WITH SPICES
(Serves 6)

1 lb Singhara fish (500 grams)
2 cloves
2 teaspoons white cumin
1″ piece cinnamon
½ teaspoon red chilli powder
½ teaspoon black pepper
Juice of half lemon
1 to 2 eggs
1½ teacups dry breadcrumbs
Ghee for deep frying
Salt to taste

Wash the fish well and dry it with a cloth. Rub salt, lemon juice, ground spices, red chilli powder and black pepper into it and keep aside for 35 minutes. Dip into beaten egg and roll in breadcrumbs. Deep fry in ghee until brown. Serve hot at dinner with potato wafers. (Fried fish with spices can be served at tea without wafers.)

TANDOORI FISH
(Serves 8)

2 lbs Hilsa fish (900 grams)
20 garlic cloves
$\frac{1}{2}$ oz ginger (15 grams)
$\frac{1}{4}$ level teaspoon ground cinnamon
3 ground cloves
1 small piece mace
3 tablespoons curd
2 teaspoons amchoor
3 teaspoons red chilli powder
$\frac{1}{2}$ teaspoon orange colour
One lemon
Salt to taste

Clean and remove the entrails of the fish and wash it. Keep
the fish whole. Dry with a clean cloth. Grind garlic and ginger
finely and then mix with ground cinnamon, cloves, mace,
amchoor, colour, salt, chilli powder and curd. Rub it into the
fish and keep aside for 15 minutes. Stick the whole fish on an
iron skewer, 2 feet long, and bake in a tandoor until dry and
tender. Now baste it frequently with ghee until light brown.
Squeeze the juice of the lemon, to taste, over the fish before
serving. Serve hot at dinner. (Hilsa fish can be grilled without
skewer in an oven on a wire rack. Baste frequently until dry
and tender. Glaze with ghee and keep it in the oven for a few
minutes.)

STUFFED POTATO SAUSAGES
(Serves 8)

12 ozs potatoes (360 grams)
16 sausages
2 teaspoons white cumin seeds
2 green chillies
A few coriander leaves
1 beaten egg
Salt to taste
Breadcrumbs for coating
Ghee for frying

Boil the potatoes in salted water till tender. Cool and grate. Mix green chillies, coriander leaves, salt and white cumin in it.

Prick the sausages and cook in 1 cup water till dry and then fry in their own fat. Fill in the grated potatoes and dip in the beaten egg and coat with breadcrumbs. Decorate with lettuce leaves, beetroot and radish. Serve at lunch or dinner.

9

CHICKEN, FISH, MUTTON AND PORK PREPARATIONS

GRILLED CHICKEN
(Serves 4)

1 chicken with skin
6 teaspoons Worcestershire sauce
½ teaspoon ajinomoto
¼ teaspoon mustard powder
1 teaspoon red chilli powder
4 teaspoons salad oil
2 teaspoons salt
Ghee for shallow frying

Cut the chicken into half. Make a paste of Worcestershire sauce, ajinomoto, chilli powder, mustard powder, salad oil and salt. Rub this into the chicken and keep it for one hour. Fry half the chicken in 3 tablespoons ghee until brown, and then fry the other half in the same way. Add ½ cup of water and cook for a few minutes. Take out the chicken from the gravy and put it on a wire rack. Put a round flat pie dish under the wire rack to catch the dripping and grill in the oven (315° F, gas mark 1-2) and turn it frequently until tender. Take out the chicken from the oven. Add the gravy into the dripping and mix well; if thick, add a little warm water and mix again. Pour it on the chicken and serve hot at lunch or dinner.

(Chicken can be grilled in a pressure cooker also. Put the chicken in a pan and cover with a lid. cook in a pressure cooker until tender. Serve hot at lunch or dinner).

CHICKEN WITH VEGETABLES
(Serves 6)

1 lb chicken (½ kg)
1 carrot
3 ozs potatoes (2 medium)
8 ozs peas (250 grams)
3 ozs cauliflower (3 medium pieces)
10 level teaspoons flour
3 teaspoons lemon juice
1 teacup cream (7 ozs)
½ teaspoon white pepper
2 to 2½ cups milk
1½ ozs butter (5 teaspoons)
½ onion
1 chopped green chilli
½ teaspoon chopped coriander leaves
2 ozs cheese
Salt to taste

Chop the vegetables and boil them in salted water. Boil the chicken with a little salt in water, until tender. Drain, remove the bones and cut into small pieces.

Fry the chopped onion and flour in butter for one minute, add milk and stir for a few minutes. Add the lemon juice, salt, pepper, chopped coriander leaves, green chillies, vegetables and chicken pieces and cook for 5 minutes. Remove from the fire,

109

add cream and ½ oz grated cheese and mix well. Pour into a greased pie dish and sprinkle the rest of the grated cheese on the top. Bake in a moderate oven (350° F, gas mark 3-4) until light brown in colour. Serve at lunch or dinner.

FISH BAKED WITH NOODLES
(Serves 8)

1 lb sole fish (½ kg)
1¼ teacups noodles
1½ ozs butter
½ cup fresh breadcrumbs

Steam the fish, remove the bones and skin and mash coarsely. Boil the noodles in salted water until tender and drain. Arrange the fish and noodles in layers in a greased dish and pour cheese sauce over the top layer. Sprinkle with soft breadcrumbs and dot with butter. Bake in a moderate oven (350° F, gas mark 3-4) until light brown. Serve hot at lunch or dinner.

Cheese sauce

1 oz butter (3 teaspoons)
1½ tablespoons flour
1 teaspoon salt
¼ teaspoon white pepper
1⅓ cups milk
1½ to 2 ozs grated cheese
½ teaspoon mustard powder

Melt the butter on a low fire, add the flour, salt and pepper and stir until light golden brown. Remove from the fire, add milk and stir. Put on the fire and cook, stirring constantly, until thick and smooth. Mix with grated cheese and mustard powder and cook until the cheese melts. Remove from the fire and pour over the fish and noodles.

FISH SOUFFLE
(Serves 8)

1 lb sole fish ($\frac{1}{2}$ kg)

$\frac{1}{2}$ teaspoon salt

$\frac{1}{4}$ teaspoon white peppeı

2 teaspoons lemon juice

$\frac{1}{2}$ cup fresh breadcrumbs

$\frac{1}{2}$ cup milk

3 egg yolks

2 egg whites

$\frac{1}{2}$ finely chopped onion

3 teaspoons finely chopped coriander leaves

Steam the fish, and remove bones and skin. Mash it coarsely and add salt, pepper, lemon juice, chopped green chillies, onion and coriander leaves. Cook the breadcrumbs in milk for a few minutes. Beat the egg yolks lightly. Add to the fish breadcrumbs cooked in milk and the beaten egg yolks. Beat the whites of eggs until stiff. Fold them lightly into the fish mixture. Grease a pie dish, pour the fish mixture in it and bake in a moderate oven (350°F gas mark 3-4) until firm. Serve with Hollandaise sauce.

HOLLANDAISE SAUCE

4 ozs butter

2 egg yolks ($\frac{1}{2}$ cup)

$\frac{1}{2}$ teaspoon salt

A pinch of red chilli powder

1 tablespoon lemon juice

1 to 2 tablespoons whipped cream

Beat the butter until creamy. Beat in the egg yolks one at a time. Add the lemon juice, salt, red chilli powder. Cook over a pan of hot water until slightly thick. Cool and mix the whipped cream. Serve with fish souffle.

111

BAKED FISH (GREECE)
(Serves 6)

6 fish slices ($\frac{1}{2}''$ thick)
5 tomatoes
4 medium onions
2 cloves garlic (minced)
$\frac{1}{2}$ cup butter
1 teaspoon salt for fish
$\frac{1}{2}$ teaspoon white pepper
3 teaspoons lemon juice
$\frac{1}{3}$ cup water
$\frac{1}{4}$ cup olive oil

Fry the minced garlic with onion slices in olive oil till slightly golden in colour. Keep aside. Rub $\frac{3}{4}$ teaspoon salt and lemon juice on the fish. Melt the butter in a baking dish and arrange the fish over it. Keep a little space between the two slices. Over and round the fish spread fried onion and tomato slices. Sprinkle with $\frac{1}{4}$ teaspoon salt, pour water over it. Bake in a moderate oven (375°F, gas mark 5-6) till the fish is tender. Serve hot.

BAKED FISH WITH CHEESE
(Serves 6)

1 lb sole or pomfret fish ($\frac{1}{2}$ kg)
3 teaspoons lemon juice
$\frac{1}{4}$ teaspoon white pepper
1 teaspoon salt for fish
$\frac{1}{4}$ cup flour for dusting
$\frac{1}{4}$ cup butter

Wash and dry the fish slices. Rub in salt, pepper and lemon juice and then dust with flour. Fry in butter till tender and slightly brown in colour. Drain on a paper and keep aside.

French sauce
$2\frac{1}{2}$ cups milk
4 teaspoons flour
1 teaspoon minced onion
5 teaspoons butter
2 teaspoons cornflour
$\frac{1}{4}$ teaspoon white pepper
$\frac{1}{2}$ cup grated cheese
1 teaspoon lemon juice
Salt to taste

Fry the flour and onion in butter till slightly brown, add the milk and cook till a little thick. Mix the cornflour in $\frac{1}{4}$ cup water and stir it in milk mixture till thick. Add salt, pepper and lemon juice. Pour a little milk mixture in a pie dish and arrange fried fish on it. Pour the rest of the milk mixture over it and sprinkle the cheese. Bake in a hot oven (375°F, gas mark 5-6) till cheese is golden brown.

MUTTON CUTLETS
(Serves 8)

1 lb keema ($\frac{1}{2}$ kg)
1 small onion
2 garlic cloves
3 chopped green chillies
2 bread slices (soaked in water and squeezed)
4 teaspoons dry breadcrumbs
1 egg
Salt to taste
Ghee for deep frying
1 teaspoon chopped coriander leaves
Breadcrumbs for coating
6 teaspoons Worcestershire sauce

Cook keema with chopped onion, garlic in 1$\frac{1}{2}$ cups water till tender and dry. Mix bread slices, green chillies, 4 teaspoons breadcrumbs, salt, Worcestershire sauce and coriander leaves. Make oval shaped cutlets, dip into beaten egg mixed with $\frac{1}{4}$ cup water and coat with breadcrumbs. Fry in ghee till golden brown. Serve at tea or breakfast.

ROASTED MUTTON LEG
(Serves 6)

1 mutton leg (2 lbs)
2 teaspoons salt
2 tablespoons ghee
2 teaspoons caramel syrup
For decoration : lettuce leaves, 2 beetroots, 2 radishes,
1 carrot and tomatoes

Fry the mutton with salt in ghee until brown. Add the caramel syrup and 2 cups water and mix well. Put in a pressure cooker and steam it until tender, or cook on a low fire in a degchi. Remove from the ghee and chill. Remove the bones, cut the meat into thin and round pieces and decorate with radish, beetroot, carrot and lettuce leaves. Sprinkle vinegar sauce on the mutton. Also serve in a separate plate lettuce leaves, round pieces of radish, tomatoes and boiled beetroot and sprinkle vinegar sauce. Serve at dinner.

Vinegar sauce
1 teaspoon mayonnaise
¼ teaspoon mustard
½ teaspoon sugar
½ teaspoon salad oil
¼ teaspoon salt
½ cup vinegar

Make a paste of salad oil, sugar, mustard powder, mayonnaise and salt, then add vinegar and mix well. Strain and sprinkle on salad and cold meat.

PORK SHASHLIK
(Serves 5)

2 pork flits or undercuts
3 big onions (sliced)
4 sliced tomatoes (without pulp)
4 green chillies
1 onion
4 small slices of fresh ginger
1 teaspoon turmeric
3 tablespoons curd
3 teaspoons salad oil
Salt to taste

Chop the onion, ginger and green chillies very finely. Mix with the curd, turmeric, salad oil, salt, chopped onion, ginger, green chillies and big pork pieces and marinate for one hour. First put onion slices on the skewer and then tomato slices and pork pieces closely. Put all the pork and vegetable pieces on 2 to 3 skewers. Roast them on a medium fire and turn frequently until dry or grill and pour 3 tablespoons salad oil, little by little, on pork pieces, until light brown. Serve hot with onion rings and tomato slices. Serve at tea or cocktail.

MAGIC SAUSAGE ROLLS
(Serves 10)

1 lb potatoes ($\frac{1}{2}$ kg)
$\frac{1}{4}$ teaspoon white pepper
1 level teaspoon salt
Dry breadcrumbs for coating
1 beaten egg
250 grams cocktail sausages
Ghee for frying

Boil the potatoes in water with $\frac{1}{2}$ teaspoon salt, till tender. Cool, peel and grate them, mix with salt and pepper and keep aside. Now prick the sausages with a fork and cook them in 1 cup water till dry and then fry them in their own fat. Fill them in grated potatoes and make into oblong shapes. Dip in beaten egg mixed with 3 teaspoons water and roll in breadcrumbs. Fry in hot ghee till golden brown. Serve at tea.

CLUB SANDWICHES
(Serves 4)

6 slices bread
2 ozs salted butter ($\frac{1}{4}$ cup)
$\frac{1}{4}$ teaspoon mustard powder
$\frac{1}{8}$ teaspoon white pepper
1 egg omelet
1 oz cooked ham ($\frac{1}{4}$ cup)
1 tomato
4 ozs boiled chicken breast (1 chicken breast)
2 ozs cashewnuts ($\frac{1}{3}$ cup)
4 ozs potatoes
2 gherkins
2 pickled onions
Ghee for frying

Cream the butter and mix mustard powder, chopped gherkins and pickled onions in it. Brown the bread slices on one side and remove the hard crusts. Spread the butter mixture on unbrowned sides. Fry the boiled chicken pieces in ghee for a few minutes. Put ham pieces, tomato slices, fried chicken, omelet and then cover with a buttered slice. Press well together. Fasten with 4 toothpicks and cut into 4 triangles. Put them on a plate and decorate with cashewnuts and potato wafers. Serve at tea.

Fry cashewnuts in a little hot ghee till light brown. Drain on paper and sprinkle salt.

Potato Wafers

Peel and cut potatoes into round and very thin slices. Soak in water for 45 minutes and dry on a clean cloth. Fry in hot ghee till golden brown, drain on paper and sprinkle salt.

118

10

DESSERTS AND SWEETS

ALMOND HALWA
(Serves 6)

8 ozs almonds (240 grams)
8 ozs ghee
2 silver leaves
4 ozs semolina (120 grams)
½ tablespoon chopped pistachios
1 lb milk (3 teacups)
4 or 5 ozs sugar (1 teacup)
6 green cardamoms

Soak the almonds overnight, peel and grind coarsely. Boil the milk with sugar until it is dissolved and keep aside. Heat the ghee, fry semolina for two minutes and add coarsely ground almonds and fry until light brown. Add the milk, crushed cardamoms and stir until thick and leaves its ghee. Remove from the fire, put in a serving dish and decorate with silver leaves and chopped pistachios. Serve hot at breakfast or tea.

SHAHI HALWA
(Serves 10)

6 ozs semolina (180 grams)
12 ozs sugar (360 grams)
1¼ pints milk (4½ teacups)
9 teaspoons flour
4 ozs khoya (120 grams)
½ ozs magaz (peeled melon seeds) (15 grams)
½ oz peeled pistachios (15 grams)
1 oz almond (30 grams)
6 green cardamoms
6 ozs ghee (180 grams)
¼ teaspoon dry yellow colour

Boil the milk, sugar and colour and stir until the sugar is dissolved. Keep it aside. Heat the ghee and fry the semolina and flour with cardamoms until a little brown. Add the milk with khoya and stir until the milk is absorbed. Then add pistachios, almonds, melon seeds and the rest of the ghee and stir until it leaves its ghee. Serve hot at dinner or lunch.

CHEESE ICE CREAM
(Serves 8)

6 cups milk (1 litre)
¾ cup sugar (120 grams)
½ cup water
1 teaspoon cornflour
¾ cup cottage cheese (60 to 70 grams)
1 teaspoon kewara flavour
¼ cup blanched almonds (30 grams)
¼ cup pistachios (15 grams)

Boil the milk until it is a little thick. Add the cornflour mixed will ½ cup milk and stir for a few minutes. Put the sugar and water in a pan and boil to a half-thread syrup. Add the grated cottage cheese and stir until sticky. Add the milk thickened with cornflour and stir for a few minutes. Remove from the fire, add chopped pistachios and almonds. Cool and add kewara flavour. Freeze it for 8 hours until set. Serve at dinner.

CHOCOLATE BURFI
(Serves 8)

12 ozs khoya (360 grams)
1 oz ghee (30 grams)
3 ozs fine sugar (90 grams)
3 or 4 teaspoons cocoa
2 silver leaves
1 tablespoon milk

Fry the khoya in ghee until dry. Add the sugar and stir till it is dissolved. Remove from the fire. Cool a little till thick and then spread half the khoya on a greased thali. Now to the rest of the khoya add cocoa and mix well (if it is too dry then add a little milk). Spread over the top of white khoya mixture. Cool and decorate with silver leaves. When set, cut into burfi shapes. Serve at tea.

ORANGE KHOYA SLICES
(Serves 10)

1 lb khoya ($\frac{1}{2}$ kg)
4 ozs castor sugar (120 grams)
2 czs orange peel (60 grams)
7 tablespoons milk
$\frac{1}{8}$ teaspoon orange colour
4 teaspoons melted ghee
A few drops orange essence

Chop the peel finely. Put the khoya, peel, milk and ghee in a heavy pan and stir on fire until dry. Add the sugar and orange colour and stir for two minutes. Remove from the fire, add orange essence and mix well. Cool a little and then make a slab of khoya with hands, and chill until set. Cut thin slices of khoya and serve at tea.

122

KHOYA GULAB JAMUN
(Serves 12)

Balls

6 ozs khoya (180 grams)

12 ozs paneer (360 grams)

4½ ozs flour (135 grams)

4½ ozs castor sugar

Ghee for frying

½ oz pistachios (15 grams)

Syrup

1 lb sugar (¾ kg)

1¼ pints water (4½ teacups)

A few drops of rose essence

2 tablespoons milk (for cleaning the syrup)

Make syrup with water and sugar. If dirty, clean with milk. Strain through a muslin cloth and leave it to cool. Knead the khoya and paneer separately till the grains disappear and they become smooth. Mix them together and knead again for about 10 minutes. Add the sifted flour and 4½ ozs of castor sugar and knead again till they are well mixed. Leave the dough covered for about 20 minutes. Make small balls and press them in the centre with the thumb and fill with two teaspoons castor sugar, ground pistachios and a little paneer and make them into balls again. Fry in hot ghee till brown and soak in the syrup for at least one hour. Boil till they are soft. Add rose essence and serve hot with syrup at tea. (Makes 40 gulab jamuns).

Paneer

3¼ pinter cow's milk (2 lit)

½ teaspoon ground citric acid

1 teacup water

Boil the milk, then take it down. Dissolve citric acid in a cup of hot water and pour gradually into the milk until it curdles. Leave for 15 minutes. Strain through a muslin cloth.

123

MUNG DAL HALWA
(Serves 8)

1 lb mung dal ($\frac{1}{2}$ kg)
10 ozs ghee (300 grams)
10 ozs milk (2$\frac{1}{2}$ teacups)
6 ozs khoya (180 grams)
10 ozs sugar (300 grams)
$\frac{1}{2}$ oz almonds (15 grams)
$\frac{1}{2}$ oz raisins (15 grams)
$\frac{1}{2}$ oz pistachios (15 grams)

Soak the mung dal in water for 6 to 8 hours. Remove the husks by washing in several changes of water. Grind it into a fine paste. Heat the ghee and fry the paste until golden brown in colour and a very agreeable fragrance is given off. Add the milk and sugar and stir for five minutes, or till thick and soft. Add the khoya and cook for one minute. Remove from the fire. Garnish with blanched and chopped almonds and pistachio nuts. Serve hot at lunch or dinner.

SUJI HALWA
(Serves 6)

4 ozs semolina

3½ ozs sugar (100 grams)

4 ozs ghee

8 ozs water (1¾ teacups)

1 oz almonds (30 grams)

1 oz raisins

5 crushed green cardamoms

Dissolve the sugar in water over fire to make a thin syrup and keep it aside. Melt the ghee in a shallow pan over low fire and add semolina and stir until it is golden in appearance. The grains of the suji swell by absorbing the ghee and a very agreeable smell is given off. Pour the sugar syrup into it. Add raisins, crushed green cardamoms an d blanched and chopped almonds. Cook till the syrup is absorbed. Remove from the fire and serve hot at lunch or tea.

WHITE PUMPKIN HALWA
(Serves 8)

4 lbs pumpkin (petha)
1 lb khoya ($\frac{1}{2}$ kg)
8 ozs ghee (250 grams)
1 teaspoon lime
6 ozs sugar (180 grams)
2 ozs blanched almonds and pistachios (60 grams)

Peel and remove the soft part of pumpkin and grate it. Put the lime in water and soak petha in it, for 10 minutes. Wash it several times until there is no taste of lime. Squeeze out the water lightly. Put the ghee, grated pumpkin and khoya in a heavy bottomed pan and stir on high fire until dry. Now add the sugar and stir until it is dissolved and leaves the sides of the pan. Remove from the fire, and put in a serving dish. Decorate with silver leaves and sprinkle chopped almonds and pistachios. Serve hot at lunch.

PUMPKIN KHEER
(Serves 8)

2 lbs buffalo milk (1 lit)
8 ozs pumpkin (250 grams)
3 ozs sugar (90 grams)
2 ozs blanched almonds and pistachios (60 grams)
4 green cardamoms

Boil the milk with green cardamoms. Add the grated pumpkin and stir until thick and the pumpkin is tender. Remove from the fire, add sugar, chopped pistachios and almonds. Serve hot or cold at lunch.

FIRNI
(Serves 12)

2½ pints milk (1½ lit)
3 ozs cornflour (90 grams)
9 ozs sugar (270 grams)
12 ozs khoya (360 grams)
Silver leaves
2 ozs almonds (60 grams)
2 ozs pistachios (60 grams)
8 big cardamoms
2 teaspoons kewara essence

Boil the milk with khoya until well mixed. Mix the cornflour in a little water and add to the milk and stir until thick. Remove from the fire, add sugar, kewara essence and mix well. Pour into 14 dessert bowls and chill until set. Decorate with silver leaves, crushed cardamoms, chopped pistachios and peeled almonds. Serve at dinner.

SHAHI TUKRI
(Serves 10)

12 slices bread

Ghee for frying

4 teacups milk

8 ozs sugar (250 grams)

½ teaspoon saffron

2 teaspoons kewara essence

8 ozs khoya (250 grams)

10 green cardamoms

4 silver leaves

1 oz almonds (30 grams)

½ oz pistachio nuts

4 cherries

Cut rectangular pieces of bread. Remove the hard crusts and fry in ghee till golden brown. Remove the slices from the ghee and keep aside. Boil the milk with crushed cardamoms and dissolve saffron and sugar in it. Soak the fried slices in milk for a few minutes. Remove the slices from milk with a flat spoon. Mix the khoya in milk and place on the fire for five minutes and add the bread slices. Cook on a low fire till the mixture thickens. Turn the slices once or twice with a flat spoon. Remove from the fire and cool a little. Add kewara essence. Place them on a serving dish. Decorate with silver leaves and sprinkle chopped almonds, pistachio nuts and cherries. Serve cold at lunch or dinner.

KULFI
(Serves 8)

4 teacups milk

3 teaspoons cornflour

1 cup khoya (115 grams)

3 green cardamoms

¼ cup chopped almonds (15 grams)

¼ cup chopped pistachios (15 grams)

¾ cup sugar (115 grams)

A few drops kewara essence

Boil the milk with crushed cardamoms. Add the khoya and stir until it becomes a little thick. Blend cornflour with a little water, and mix it with milk. Remove from the fire, add sugar, peeled and chopped almonds, pistachio nuts and kewara. Cool and fill in kulfi moulds. Place in freezing chamber to set for 8 hours. Serve with faluda.

FALUDA

½ cup arrowroot (25 grams)

2 cups water

Mix the arrowroot with water and strain. Put it on the fire and stir until it becomes thick. Put iced water in a pail and on it keep faluda machine. Put arrowroot mixture in it and press it. Take out the faluda from the pail and put in the dish and pour ½ cup of cold water on it. Serve faluda on top of kulfi and sprinkle thin syrup and kewara essence.

Ingredients: Faluda syrup

⅓ cup sugar (60 grams)

1 cup water

2 teaspoons kewara essence

Boil sugar and water. When it becomes a little sticky remove from the fire. Cool and mix kewara. Sprinkle on the faluda. (Faluda can be taken without kulfi in iced milk sweetened with sugar and flavoured with kewara.)

MANGO KULFI
(Serves 8)

4 teacups milk
1 tablespoon cornflour
1 teacup khoya (115 grams)
¾ teacup sugar
¾ teacup thin mango slices

Boil the milk with khoya and stir until it becomes a little thick. Blend the cornflour with a little water and add it to the milk mixture until it becomes thick. Add mango slices and sugar and cook for a few minutes until sugar is dissolved. Remove from the fire and cool. Fill in kulfi moulds and freeze. Time taken for freezing is 8 hours. Serve at lunch or dinner.

VANILLA ICE CREAM
(Serves 8)

1½ teacups milk
¾ cup sugar
⅛ teaspoon salt
1½ tablespoons flour
1½ cups cream
½ teaspoon vanilla essence

Boil the milk. Make a paste of flour, sugar and salt with a little milk. Stir into the rest of the milk and cook over a low fire, stirring constantly, till thick. Cool and pour into a 10 oz tin. Freeze until a little set. Put the frozen mixture into a bowl and beat it with an egg beater. Mix colour, essence and whipped cream. Line the tin with wax paper. Pour the mixture in it and cover it to freeze until set.

COCONUT BURFI
(Serves 12)

1 lb khoya (½ kg)
8 ozs castor sugar (240 grams)
3 ozs grated coconut (90 grams)
1 to 2 tablespoons water
A few drops of red colour
Silver leaves

Put the khoya and water in a karahi and stir for 5 minutes on the fire. Add the sugar and stir till it is dissolved and khoya is a little dry. Remove from the fire, cool a little and mix grated coconut. Take half the mixture and add red colour mixed with a little water. Spread the white khoya on a greased plate and spread pink coloured khoya on the top.

MAL PURA
(Serves 8)

2½ pints milk (1½ lit)
3¼ ozs flour (100 grams)
4 ozs milk (¾ teacup)
½ oz chopped pistachios (15 grams)
¼ oz chopped almonds (7 grams)
Ghee for shallow frying
1½ lbs sugar (680 grams)
1¼ pints water (4½ teacups)

Stir the milk on fire until thick (pouring consistency), and cool. Mix the flour and 4 ozs milk and add the thickened milk. Put the sugar and water on fire until a sticky syrup is formed. Remove from the fire. Heat ghee in a frying pan and pour the milk and flour mixture one spoonful at a time and flatten it. When one side is browned turn it over and take it out immediately so that the other side does not become brown. Immerse them in warm syrup for a few minutes, then take out. Makes 16 or 18 puras. Put in a serving plate and sprinkle chopped pistachios and almonds on browned side of mal puras. Serve hot at breakfast.

BAKED FRUIT PUDDING
(Serves 8)

6 teaspoons condensed milk

5 ozs flour (150 grams)

1 teaspoonful baking powder

¼ teaspoonful soda bicarbonate

2 ozs butter 60 grams)

5 ozs milk (1 teacup)

Pinch of salt

1 teaspoon vanilla essence

¼ teaspoon yellow colour

3 bananas

1 orange

1 apple

8 to 10 ozs cream (1½ teacups)

1½ ozs castor sugar (45 grams)

¼ ozs pistachios (7 grams)

½ teaspoon red colour

1 teaspoon strawberry essence

Beat the melted butter, condensed milk, colour, milk and essence. Mix the sifted flour, baking powder, soda bicarbonate and salt with the milk mixture. Pour into a round mould, greased and dusted with flour, and bake in a moderate oven (350°F, gas mark 3-4). Cool and slit horizontally into two layers. Lift the top layer. Whip the cream with red colour, strawberry essence and castor sugar until a little thick. Spread the cream on the bottom layer, put chopped fruit and cover with cream and then with the pudding layer. Now decorate the top of the pudding with cream and chopped pistachios. Leave it for 15 minutes to set and serve it at lunch or dinner.

133

FRUIT FLAN PUDDING
(Serves 8)

5 ozs flour (150 grams)
2 ozs ghee (60 grams)
A pinch of salt
Cold water for mixing
1 tin fruit cocktail
1 teaspoon arrowroot
5 to 6 ozs cream (1 teacup)
Cherry for decoration
A few drops of yellow colour
½ oz sugar (15 grams)
A few drops of vanilla essence

Sift the flour and salt together. Rub the ghee into the flour with the fingertips until the mixture looks like fine breadcrumbs. Mix with cold water to a stiff dough. Turn onto a board and knead it lightly till free from cracks. Roll it out to the size of the dish ⅛ inch thick. Place over the rolling pin and put into the pie dish. Roll the rolling pin over the top of the pie dish and trim the edges with a knife. Make leaves from the leftover dough and decorate the flan. Prick the centre of the flan to prevent it from rising and cover with a piece of butter paper and put in a few dry beans or rice on the paper and bake for 10 minutes at 425°F, gas mark 5-6, or until cooked. Remove the paper with beans and again put in the oven for five minutes to dry. Remove from the oven and cool.

To fill the flan case strain the fruit, and arrange in the cold baked flan case. Mix arrowroot with ½ cup of cold water. Heat the fruit juice and pour arrowroot mixture into it and cook until the sauce clears; add yellow colour, vanilla essence and ½ oz of sugar. Pour over the fruit, cool and decorate with whipped cream mixed with yellow colour. Place the cherry in the centre. Serve at dinner. (Decorate with rosette tube.)

ALMOND CAKE
(Serves 6)

2 tablespoon condensed milk

5 ozs flour (150 grams)

$\frac{1}{4}$ teaspoon salt

$2\frac{1}{2}$ ozs peeled and ground almonds (75 grams)

4 to 5 ozs milk (1 teacup)

1 teaspoon baking powder

$\frac{1}{4}$ teaspoon soda bicarbonate

2 ozs butter 60 grams)

$\frac{1}{4}$ teaspoon yellow colour

$\frac{1}{4}$ teaspoon lemon essence

$\frac{1}{4}$ teaspoon almond essence

Beat the melted butter, condensed milk, milk and essence and then mix sifted flour, salt, soda, baking powder and crushed almonds. Grease a round cake tin and dust it with flour. Pour the mixture in it and bake in a hot oven (375°F, gas mark 5-6). Cool and sprinkle icing sugar.

PLUM CAKE
(Serves 8)

8 ozs flour (240 grams)

½ level teaspoon salt

2 teaspoons baking powder

1 teaspoon bicarbonate of soda

¼ teaspoon grated nutmeg

1 ½ lbs fruit peels—cherries, blanched almonds, raisins (¾ kg)

4 ozs butter (120 grams)

½ tablespoon caramel syrup

10 ozs milk (2 teacups)

2 ozs sugar (60 grams)

½ tin condensed milk

Sift the flour, salt, baking powder, soda and nutmeg together. Cream the butter and sugar, then add sifted ingredients and mix well. Add the fruit, condensed milk, caramel syrup and milk and mix to a fairly soft consistency. Line a cake tin with brown paper and grease it. Pour the mixture into it and bake in a moderate oven (gas mark 3-4). This cake can be kept for 2 weeks. (For caramel syrup heat 1 teaspoon sugar in a frying pan on a low fire till brown, add ½ cup water and stir till lumps are dissolved.)

SMALL FRUIT CAKES

(Serves 8)

4 ozs condensed milk ($\frac{1}{4}$ tin)

5 ozs milk (8 teacup)

5 ozs flour (150 grams)

1 teaspoonful baking powder

2 ozs butter (60 grams)

$\frac{1}{4}$ teaspoon soda bicarbonate

A pinch of salt

1 teaspoon strawberry essence

1 oz preserved petha (30 grams)

$\frac{1}{4}$ oz cherries

$\frac{1}{4}$ oz raisins

$\frac{1}{2}$ teaspoon yellow colour

Beat the condensed milk, milk, melted butter, essence and yellow colour. Add shifted flour, soda bicarbonate, salt and baking powder and mix well. Wash the fruit, dry on a cloth and dust it with flour. Mix this fruit with the cake mixture. Grease 3 small square moulds and dust with flour. Pour the cake mixture into these moulds. Bake in a moderate oven (350°F, gas mark 3-4). Cool and keep in an airtight tin and serve at tea.

WALNUT CHOCOLATE CAKE

(Serves 8)

3 $\frac{1}{2}$ or 4 ozs condensed milk ($\frac{1}{3}$ tin)

5 ozs flour (150 grams)

$\frac{1}{2}$ oz to $\frac{3}{4}$ oz cocoa (15 grams)

1 teaspoon baking powder

$\frac{1}{4}$ teaspoon soda bicarbonate

2 ozs butter (60 grams)

$\frac{1}{2}$ teaspoon vanilla essence

5 ozs milk (1 teacup)

A pinch of salt

Sift the flour, cocoa, baking powder and soda. Beat the milk, melted butter, condensed milk and essence. Add the sifted ingredients and mix well. Grease a round tin and dust with flour. Pour the mixture in it and bake in a moderate oven (350⁰F, gas mark 3-4). Keep in an airtight box for 4 to 6 hours. Cut into 3 layers and spread yellow, white and chocolate icing separately on each layer.

White butter icing

90 grams butter

$\frac{3}{4}$ teacup icing sugar

$\frac{1}{2}$ teaspoon vanilla essence

1 $\frac{1}{2}$ tablespoons lukewarm water

2 teaspoon cocoa

Cream the butter and icing sugar. add vanilla essence, cocoa and water and beat well until smooth.

Chocolate icing

1 cup icing sugar

2 to 3 teaspoons water

Tiny knob of butter

¼ oz cocoa (1 teaspoon)
¾ cup walnuts

Put all the ingredients in a bowl and stir over a pan of hot water until they turn into liquid. Pour on the cake and leave it to set. Coat the sides with coarsely ground walnuts.

Yellow butter icing
4 ozs icing sugar (¾ teacup)
1 oz butter (30 grams)
A few drops yellow colour

Mix all the ingredients well and then decorate the cake with it.

BREAD PUDDING
(Serves 8)

10 bread slices
2 cups milk
2 eggs
½ cup sugar
1 teaspoon kewara essence
Jam or jelly
⅛ cup butter

Spread butter and jam on the slices. Arrange in a greased pudding dish. Beat the eggs, milk, sugar and kewara essence together and pour over the slices and keep till the liquid is absorbed. Bake (350ºF, gas mark 3-4) till golden brown. Serve hot.

INDIAN ROYAL PUDDING
(Serves 6)

4 ozs khoya ($\frac{3}{4}$ cup)

2 eggs

4 ozs sugar ($\frac{3}{4}$ cup)

3 ozs ghee ($\frac{1}{3}$ cup)

2 ozs flour ($\frac{1}{2}$ cup)

$\frac{1}{2}$ teaspoon baking powder

1 teaspoon kewara essence

2 teaspoons almonds

1 teaspoon pistachios

2 teaspoons raisins

Cream the chilled ghee and sugar until fluffy, add yolks of eggs and beat. Mix the mashed khoya, sifted flour and baking powder. Beat the egg whites until stiff. Mix peeled and chopped almonds, raisins, pistachios and kewara essence with the egg mixture and lastly fold in the egg whites lightly. Grease a loaf tin and dust with flour. Pour the mixture in it but do not fill it more than two-thirds. Bake in a moderate oven (350°F, gas mark 3-4), about 45 minutes, until light brown. Cool and turn out onto a dish. Pour hot cornflour custard on the baked pudding and cover it.

Custard

10 ozs milk (2 cups)

1$\frac{1}{2}$ ozs sugar ($\frac{1}{3}$ cup)

$\frac{1}{4}$ teaspoon salt

A few drops yellow colour

2 egg yolks

2 teaspoons cornflour

$\frac{1}{2}$ teaspoon kewara essence

5 ozs cream ($\frac{3}{4}$ cup)

Pistachios for decoration

Make a paste of sugar, salt, cornflour and eggs. Boil the milk,

140

then lower the heat. Add the paste of cornflour into the milk and stir until thick. Remove from the fire. Mix half the cream and kewara essence. Pour it while hot on the pudding and cool it. Now whip the rest of the cream with yellow colour and decorate the custard with it. Sprinkle chopped pistachios.

BAKED APPLES IN HANDKERCHIEF
(Serves 8)

Short crust

6 ozs flour (1½ cups)
2 level teaspoons baking powder
¼ teaspoon salt
6 teaspoons castor sugar
9 teaspoons butter
¾ cup milk

Sift the flour, baking powder, salt and sugar. Mix the butter into the sifted ingredients with fingertips. Add the milk to make a soft dough, and keep it in a cool place for 5 minutes. Roll it out ½ inch thick and cut into 4 squares.

Apples

4 medium apples
2 ozs brown sugar (8 teaspoons)
¼ oz butter (1½ teaspoons)
½ teaspoon cinnamon powder
2 teaspoons ground cashewnuts
2 to 3 teaspoons lemon juice

Peel and core the apples. Fill the hollows of apples with the mixture of brown sugar, cinnamon powder and cashewnuts. Sprinkle the lemon juice on brown sugar and dot with butter.

Put each apple on a square of short crust dough. Bring opposite corners of the dough together on top of the apples. Wet the edges of the sides with water and seal them. Prick the covering with a knife to prevent it from rising. Bake in a moderate oven (375°F, gas mark 5-6) for about 40 minutes or until apples are tender and short crust is brown. Pour lemon sauce over the baked apples and serve hot.

Lemon sauce

4 ozs sugar (¾ cup)

3 teaspoons cornflour

1½ cups water

1 oz butter (2 teaspoons)

½ teaspoon cinnamon powder

2 tablespoons lemon juice

¼ teaspoon salt

¼ teaspoon yellow colour

Mix the cornflour, salt and sugar together and stir into boiling water. Cook on a low fire until a little thick. Remove from the fire, add lemon juice, cinnamon powder, yellow colour and butter. Pour on baked apples.

CARAMEL CUSTARD
(Serves 6)

3 big eggs

2 cups milk

¼ cup water

⅓ cup sugar

½ teaspoon vanilla essence

Melt ¼ cup sugar in a steaming mould till brown in colour. Cover the sides of the mould with caramel syrup. Beat the eggs, sugar, milk and essence and pour the mixture over the caramel. Steam it very gently for 45 minutes or until the mixture is firm. Cool and keep it for one hour and turn it out on-to a dish. Serve at lunch or dinner.

(CREPES SUZETTE FRENCH)

2 ozs sifted flour ($\frac{1}{2}$ cup)

$\frac{1}{2}$ teaspoon sugar

$\frac{1}{2}$ teaspoon salt

1 teaspoon baking powder

1 teaspoon lemon juice

1 tablespoon milk

Ghee for frying

7 tablespoons water

Mix all the ingredients and beat to a dropping consistency. Strain and keep for one hour. Heat some ghee and pour a little mixture in it and spread it evenly. Cook until set. Turn it over, and keep it on fire until light brown. Repeat this process until all the mixture is finished. Cover the pan cakes with a wet cloth to prevent drying.

Orange sauce

2 cups orange juice

$\frac{1}{4}$ teaspoon salt

2 tablespoons lemon juice

$\frac{1}{2}$ cup sugar

1 oz butter (3 teaspoons)

3 tablespoons brandy or any wine

1 teaspoon orange extract

Put the orange juice, salt, lemon juice and butter in a pan and boil. Add the sugar and stir until it is dissolved. Remove from the fire, put pan cakes, one by one, in it and prick with a fork and turn over. Put in a serving dish and sprinkle heated orange extract and wine. Light with a match. Serve immediately.

CHOCOLATE BREAD PUDDING

(Serves 6)

1 cup milk (5 ozs)

2 cups fresh breadcrumbs

1½ ozs melted butter (5 teaspoons)

2 ozs sugar (⅓ cup)

2 eggs

⅛ teaspoon salt

1½ ozs raisins (¼ cup)

4 cherries

½ Vanilla essence teaspoon cinnamon powder

2 teaspoons cocoa

Boil the milk. Pour over fresh breadcrumbs and cool. Mix melted butter, sugar, cocoa, salt, slightly beaten egg yolks, raisins, cinnamon powder or vanilla essence with a wire beater. Pour into a buttered pie dish and set in a pan of hot water (2″ deep). Bake in a moderate oven (350° F, gas mark 5-6) for about one hour. Decorate the pudding with meringue. Serve hot with lightly whipped cream.

Meringue

2 egg whites

2 ozs sugar (¼ cup)

2 teaspoons cocoa

A few cherry pieces

Whip the egg whites till stiff. Mix the sugar (keep 2 teaspoons for sprinkling on the meringue) and cocoa. Spread the beaten egg whites over the baked pudding and sprinkle small pieces of cherries and 2 teaspoons sugar. Bake till crisp.

CHRISTMAS PUDDING
(Serves 8)

1 cup fresh breadcrumbs

¼ cup butter

2 teaspoons instant coffee

2 teaspoons caramel syrup

¼ teaspoon soda bicarbonate

1 teaspoon baking powder

2 eggs

¼ cup rum

½ teaspoon ground cinnamon

¼ teaspoon ground nutmeg

¼ teaspoon ground cloves

½ cup raisins

½ cup pitted chopped dates

½ cup chopped seedless sultanas

¼ cup mixed peel

¼ teaspoon salt

Cream the butter with sugar. Add the eggs and beat again. Mix baking powder, soda bicarbonate, all the spices, salt, chopped dry fruits, fresh breadcrumbs, rum, caramel syrup and coffee. Grease a steaming mould with butter and fill it three-fourths with the mixture. Steam for about 2 hours till set and a little firm. Serve hot with 1 cup whipped cream. (This pudding can be kept for 3 weeks. Just before serving, heat it in the same mould in which pudding is steamed.)

HOT SOUFFLE

(Serves 8)

2 ozs butter (6 teaspoons)

6 ozs flour (1½ teacups)

¼ teaspoon salt

1 cup milk

3 eggs

½ teaspoon vanilla essence

1 teaspoon cream of tartar

4 ozs sugar (¾ cup)

2 ozs cashewnuts (⅓ cup)

5 teaspoons icing sugar

1 cup cream

¼ teaspoon vanilla essence for cream

Melt the butter and add flour, milk and salt and stir it on fire, till thick and smooth. Beat the egg yolks and sugar till frothy. Mix the flour mixture with yolk mixture and vanilla essence. Beat the egg whites and cream of tartar till stiff. Mix it lightly with yolks and flour mixture. Pour into a greased pie dish, sprinkle with cashewnuts and bake it over a pan of hot water (350° F, gas mark 4-5) till it is risen and golden brown. Remove from the oven and serve hot with lightly whipped cream mixed with ¼ teaspoon vanilla essence and icing sugar. Serve at lunch or dinner. (If the milk mixture becomes thick after cooking, add a little more milk and mix it well.)

FRUIT GATEAU PUDDING (FRENCH)
(Serves 6)

2 eggs

2 ozs sugar ($\frac{1}{3}$ cup)

2 ozs flour ($\frac{1}{2}$ cup)

2 tablespoons water

$\frac{1}{2}$ teaspoon strawberry essence

$\frac{1}{4}$ teaspoon raspberry red colour

1 cherry

8 to 10 ozs cream (2 teacups)

2 ozs castor sugar ($\frac{1}{3}$ cup)

2 apples

2 pineapple slices

Beat the eggs, sugar and water over a pan of hot water until frothy. Add essence and colour and mix well. Fold the sifted flour lightly. Grease the mould and dust it with flour. Pour the mixture in it and bake in a moderate oven (350° F, gas mark 4-5). Cool and cut into two layers. Whip the cream with sugar, $\frac{1}{4}$ teaspoon essence and red colour. Keep half the cream for decoration and to the remaining portion add chopped fruit. Spread the fruit and cream on the layers of cake and decorate the top with cream and cherry. Serve at lunch or dinner.

ICEBERG PUDDING
(Serves 8)

3 eggs (5 small)

2 teaspoons cornflour

4 ozs sugar ($\frac{3}{4}$ cup)

1$\frac{1}{2}$ level teaspoons gelatine

1 tablespoon hot water

1 pint milk (3$\frac{1}{2}$ cups)

5 ozs cream

$\frac{1}{2}$ teaspoon vanilla essence

6 ozs grapes (1 cup)

1 to 2 bananas

1 teaspoon dry grated coconut

4 cherries

A few drops red colour

2 ozs castor sugar ($\frac{1}{3}$ cup)

Beat the egg yolks and sugar with a wooden spoon and mix with the boiled and cooled milk. Cook over a pan of hot water on a low fire, stirring constantly, until it coats the spoon. Remove from the fire and stir for five minutes. Cool and mix lightly whipped cream and the fruit and pour into ice cream cups. Beat the egg whites until stiff. Mix vanilla essence and gelatine dissolved in hot water, drop by drop, and beat it. Now fold in castor sugar gradually. Drop the meringue on the custard and decorate with chopped cherries and coloured coconut and chill it again till the meringue sets. Serve at lunch or dinner.

CHOCOLATE CREAM BISCUITS
(Serves 8)

4 ozs butter ($\frac{3}{4}$ cup)

3 ozs castor sugar ($\frac{1}{2}$ cup)

2 eggs

8 ozs flour (2 cups)

$\frac{1}{4}$ teaspoon vanilla essence

$\frac{1}{4}$ teaspoon baking powder

Cream the butter and sugar until fluffy. Add the eggs and vanilla essence and beat. Put the sifted flour, baking powder on a wooden board and mix with the egg mixture lightly. If the dough is too soft, add more flour and mix well. Roll out $\frac{1}{8}''$ thick and cut it with a round biscuit cutter. Bake in a moderate oven (350° F, gas mark 3-4) until light brown and cool. Join two biscuits together with chocolate butter icing. Decorate with hard chocolate icing.

Chocolate butter icing

2 ozs butter (6 teaspoons)

1 teaspoon cocoa

2 ozs castor sugar ($\frac{1}{3}$ cup)

A little water

Icing sugar

Cream the butter and sugar until fluffy and mix cocoa in it. If too thick, add a little water to make it soft. Spread it on the biscuits. Decorate the top of biscuits with it and sprinkle some icing sugar. For thick chocolate icing, take a little chocolate butter icing and mix 1 teaspoon cocoa in it.

LEMON AND ALMOND COOKIES
(Serves 12)

6 ozs flour (1½ teacups)
¼ teaspoon salt
3 ozs butter
3 ozs ghee (9 teaspoons)
1 or 2 eggs
1 oz sugar (⅛ teacup)
A few drops of each lemon and almond essence
2 ozs blanched almonds

Cream the butter, ghee and sugar. Beat the egg and essence in it. Sift the flour and salt together and mix with the creamed mixture. Make 2½ dozen cookies in fancy shapes with a rosette tube and bake on baking tray lined with brown paper. Decorate with coarsely ground almonds. Chill on ice. Bake in a moderate oven (350° F, gas mark 3-4) until light brown. Cool and serve at tea.

COFFEE PASTRY
(Serves 12)

3 eggs
3 ozs sugar ($\frac{1}{2}$ cup)
3 ozs flour ($\frac{3}{4}$ cup)
1 teaspoon coffee essence

Beat the eggs and sugar in a bowl over a pan of hot water until frothy. Mix the sifted flour lightly and add the coffee essence. Pour into a baking tray greased and dusted with flour. Bake in a moderate oven (350° F, gas mark 3-4). Cool and cut into two layers and spread butter icing on it.

Butter icing

$\frac{1}{4}$ cup butter
$\frac{1}{2}$ cup icing sugar
$\frac{1}{2}$ teaspoon vanilla essence
Apricot Jam

Cream the butter and icing sugar and mix the essence. Spread it on the layer of pastry and keep in fridge for 15 minutes. Cut the pastry into medium-sized pieces and spread a little apricot jam over them.

Coffee icing

$1\frac{1}{2}$ cups icing sugar
3 to 4 teaspoons water
1 teaspoon butter
2 teaspoons coffee essence

Put all the ingredients in a degchi except the coffee essence and melt on a low fire over a pan of hot water until it becomes liquid. Mix the coffee essence and pour over the pastry.

151

CHOCOLATE CAKE
(Serves 6)

3 ozs flour ($\frac{3}{4}$ cup)

3 teaspoons cocoa

3 ozs sugar ($\frac{1}{4}$ cup)

3 eggs

Sieve the flour and cocoa together. Put the eggs and sugar in a basin and whisk over a pan of hot water till thick and frothy. Fold in the sifted flour and cocoa lightly. Put this mixture in a greased square tin and bake in a moderate oven. Remove from the tin, cool on a wire rack. Cut into two layers and fill with chocolate cream icing. Cut two thin slices from the cake for cake crumbs.

Chocolate cream icing

$2\frac{1}{2}$ ozs butter ($\frac{1}{2}$ cup)

$1\frac{1}{2}$ ozs castor sugar ($\frac{1}{3}$ cup)

2 teaspoons cocoa

3 teaspoons cold water

Beat the butter, sugar, cocoa and water till smooth and creamy. Use this chocolate cream icing on the layers, sides and top of the cake. Coat the sides with cake crumbs.